8th Meeting of the ACL Special Interest Group on Computational Phonology 2006

(SIGPHON 2006)

Held at HLT/NAACL 2006

New York, New York, USA
8 June 2006

ISBN: 978-1-61738-490-5

Printed from e-media with permission by:

Curran Associates, Inc.
57 Morehouse Lane
Red Hook, NY 12571
www.proceedings.com

Some format issues inherent in the e-media version may also appear in this print version.

Printed by Curran Associates, Inc. (2010)

Association for Computational Linguistics
209 N. Eighth Street
Stroudsburg, Pennsylvania 18360

Phone: 1-570-476-8006
Fax: 1-570-476-0860

acl@aclweb.org

Introduction

We are pleased to present the Proceedings of the Eighth Meeting of the ACL Special Interest Group on Computational Phonology (SIGPHON) to be held on June 8 in New York City. This is the first time that the SIGPHON workshop has been collocated with the HLT-NAACL conference. Previous meetings were held in conjunction with ACL and COLING in Las Cruces (1994), Santa Cruz (1996), Madrid (1997), Quebec (1998), Luxembourg (2000), Philadelphia (2002), and Barcelona (2004).

One of the missions of SIGPHON is to encourage interaction between work in computational linguistics and work in theoretical phonology, in the hope that both fields will profit from the interaction. In addition, SIGPHON continues to promote work in computational morphology, seeking to fill in for the absence of an analogous SIGMORPH group. Our recent meetings have been successful in both regards, and we anticipate this will continue in 2006. Many mainstream phonologists are employing computational tools and models that are of considerable interest to computational linguists more generally, and our intention is that this workshop should be a forum to bring this work to the attention of a wider range of computational linguists.

The submissions were reviewed by a program committee composed of eighteen experts in the field. We are grateful to them for their timely, thoughtful, and thorough reviews.

We hope you enjoy this year's meeting!

Greg Kondrak
Richard Wicentowski
June 2006

Organizers:

Richard Wicentowski, Swarthmore College
Greg Kondrak, University of Alberta

SIGPHON Executive Committee:

Jason Eisner, The Johns Hopkins University, President
Richard Wicentowski, Swarthmore College, Secretary
Adam Albright, Massachusetts Institute of Technology
Katrin Kirchoff, University of Washington
Eric Fosler-Lussier, The Ohio State University

Program Committee Members:

Adam Albright, University of California, Santa Cruz
Paul Boersma, University of Amsterdam
Anja Belz, University of Brighton
Steven Bird, University of Melbourne
Julie Carson-Berndsen, University College Dublin
John Coleman, University of Oxford
Mathias Creutz, Helsinki University of Technology
Jason Eisner, The Johns Hopkins University
John Goldsmith, University of Chicago
Sharon Goldwater, Brown University
Lauri Karttunen, Palo Alto Research Center
Greg Kondrak, University of Alberta
Mike Maxwell, Linguistic Data Consortium
Kemal Oflazer, Sabanci University
Gerald Penn, University of Toronto
Vito Pirrelli, Istituto di Linguistica Computazionale
Jason Riggle, University of Chicago
Richard Sproat, University of Illinois at Urbana-Champaign

Workshop Website:

`http://nlp.cs.swarthmore.edu/sigphon06/`

Table of Contents

Conference Program

Thursday, June 8, 2006

9:00–9:30	*A Combined Phonetic-Phonological Approach to Estimating Cross-Language Phoneme Similarity in an ASR Environment* Lynette Melnar and Chen Liu
9:30–10:00	*Improving Syllabification Models with Phonotactic Knowledge* Karin Müller
10:00–10:30	*Learning Quantity Insensitive Stress Systems via Local Inference* Jeffrey Heinz
10:30–11:00	Break
11:00–12:30	Invited Talk: *Universal Constraint Rankings Result from Learning and Evolution* Paul Boersma
12:30–14:00	Lunch
14:00–14:30	*Exploring variant definitions of pointer length in MDL* Aris Xanthos, Yu Hu and John Goldsmith
14:30–15:00	*Improved morpho-phonological sequence processing with constraint satisfaction inference* Antal van den Bosch and Sander Canisius
15:00–15:30	*Richness of the Base and Probabilistic Unsupervised Learning in Optimality Theory* Gaja Jarosz
15:30–16:00	Break
16:00–16:30	*Morphology Induction from Limited Noisy Data Using Approximate String Matching* Burcu Karagol-Ayan, David Doermann and Amy Weinberg
16:30–17:00	*Learning Probabilistic Paradigms for Morphology in a Latent Class Model* Erwin Chan
17:00–17:30	*A Naive Theory of Affixation and an Algorithm for Extraction* Harald Hammarström

A Combined Phonetic-Phonological Approach to Estimating Cross-Language Phoneme Similarity in an ASR Environment

Lynette Melnar
lynette.melnar@motorola.com

Chen Liu
chen.liu@motorola.com

Abstract

This paper presents a fully automated linguistic approach to measuring distance between phonemes across languages. In this approach, a phoneme is represented by a feature matrix where feature categories are fixed, hierarchically related and binary-valued; feature categorization explicitly addresses allophonic variation and feature values are weighted based on their relative prominence derived from lexical frequency measurements. The relative weight of feature values is factored into phonetic distance calculation. Two phonological distances are statistically derived from lexical frequency measurements. The phonetic distance is combined with the phonological distances to produce a single metric that quantifies cross-language phoneme distance.

The performances of target-language phoneme HMMs constructed solely with source language HMMs, first selected by the combined phonetic and phonological metric and then by a data-driven, acoustics distance-based method, are compared in context-independent automatic speech recognition (ASR) experiments. Results show that this approach consistently performs equivalently to the acoustics-based approach, confirming its effectiveness in estimating cross-language similarity between phonemes in an ASR environment.

1 Introduction

Speech technologists typically use acoustic measurements to determine similarity among acoustic speech models (phone(me) HMMs) and there are a variety of distance metrics available that prove the effectiveness of this method (see Sooful and Botha 2002). Additionally, HMM similarity can be evaluated indirectly through comparison of HMM performances in ASR experiments.

For acoustic measurements, speech data must be accessible for model training. However, speech data unavailability is a practical concern in that most commercially available speech databases are restricted to widely spoken languages in large business markets. The vast majority of languages have not been exposed to intense data collection and resources for these languages are subsequently either limited or completely unavailable. Hence a knowledge-based phoneme distance metric potentially has great value in acoustic modeling for resource-limited languages in that it can predict cross-language HMM similarity in the absence of target-language speech data.

Knowledge-based approaches to HMM similarity generally attempt to identify articulatory similarity between phonemes across languages. The typical strategy is subjective and label-based, where two phonemes are judged to be more or less similar depending on their transcription labels (Köhler 1996; Schultz and Waibel 1997, 2000).

A label-based approach suffers for two obvious reasons. First, phone inventories designed for speech technology applications are predominantly phonemic in orientation. Thus, transcription labels do not transfer with the same phonetic value to other languages, even where international phonetic transcription labels are employed. In a phonemic transcription strategy, transcription labels are gen-

Proceedings of the Eighth Meeting of the ACL Special Interest Group on Computational Phonology at HLT-NAACL 2006, pages 1–10,
New York City, USA, June 2006.

erally restricted to only the most basic symbols, usually unmodified letters of the Roman alphabet (IPA 1999). Second, phoneme transcription labels fail to capture allophony. The best phonetic definition that a phoneme transcription label can offer is the most typical phonetic realization of that phoneme. Not surprisingly, label-based cross-language transfer experiments have produced poor performance results.

In contrast to the subjective, label-based strategy, researchers in such fields as language reconstruction, dialectometry, and child language development, commonly use automatic feature-based approaches to articulatory similarity between phonemes. In these methods, phonemes are represented by a distinctive feature vector and a phonetic distance or similarity algorithm is used to align phoneme strings between related words (Connolly 1997; Kessler 1995, 2005; Kondrak 2002; Nerbonne and Heeringa 1997; Somers 1998). Significantly, in these approaches, phonological similarity is generally assumed.

In principle, the feature-based approach to phonetic distance admits more precise specification of phonemes because it supports allophonic variance. For example, a standard feature-based approach to allophony representation restricts feature inclusion to only those features relevant to all realizations of the phoneme. Another common approach retains features that are relevant to all allophonic variants, but leaves their values underspecified (Archangeli 1988). However, it is unclear from the literature whether allophony is explicitly addressed in the current feature-based approaches to phoneme similarity.

A strategy for specifying allophony and characterizing phonetic distance between phonemes is only one component in predicting phoneme similarity among diverse languages without acoustic data in an ASR environment. Because HMMs represent phonemes and significant allophones in a language-dependent context, it is necessary to consider the overall constructed target-language HMM system. Thus phonological distance quantities that regulate the priority of source languages for phoneme selection in accordance to their phonological similarity to the target language are also in order.

In this paper, we describe an automated, combined phonetic-phonological (CPP) approach to estimating phoneme similarity across languages in ASR. Elsewhere, we provide the phonetic and phonological distance algorithms (Liu and Melnar 2005, 2006), though offer little linguistic justification of the approach or evaluation of the experiment results due to space limitations. Here, we focus on explaining the linguistic principles behind the algorithms and analyzing the results.

The CPP approach is fundamentally based on articulatory phonetic features and is designed to handle allophonic variation. Feature salience and phonetic distance are automatically calculated and phoneme distance is constrained by statistically-derived phonological similarity biases. Unlike other distinctive feature-based approaches to phoneme similarity, phonological distance is *not* assumed. In testing this approach in cross-language transfer experiments, target-language resources are restricted to lexica and phonology descriptions and do not include speech data.

In the next section, we describe our feature-based phoneme specification method. In section three, we show how our phoneme specification approach is used in calculating phonetic distance between phonemes. Section four describes two other distance metrics that predict phonological similarity between languages. We explain how the three distance metrics combine to quantify cross-language phoneme distance and select target-language phoneme HMM inventories. In section five, we describe the experiments that we conducted to evaluate our approach to phoneme similarity prediction. Here, the CPP method is compared with an acoustic distance method in context-independent speech recognition. We offer our evaluation and conclusions in section 6.

2 Phoneme specification

In the CPP approach to estimating cross-language phoneme similarity, each phoneme in our multilingual ASR dataset is associated with a distinctive feature matrix. Feature categories are fixed for all phonemes, hierarchically related, and binary-valued. Feature-contradiction, associated with allophonic variance, is explicitly addressed through the introduction of a small set of special corollary features.

2.1 The phoneme feature matrix

As noted in the introduction, cross-language phoneme comparison requires accurate feature specification. Because a phoneme comprises one or more allophones which may contrast in particular features, a distinctive feature strategy that allows for feature contradiction is preferred. Omitting contradictory features and underspecifying contradictory values are two well-known methods.

However, cross-language phoneme comparison in a computational environment is greatly facilitated by agreeing on a *fixed* set of *binary-valued* features for all phonemes. A fixed set of distinctive features is favored as this enables cross-class phoneme comparison. A binary-valued system is easy to manipulate and naturally lends itself to mathematical formulation. However, strict binary-valued feature systems only indicate the presence or absence of a feature, and feature contradiction must then be indicated by feature omission - which is not possible in a fixed distinctive feature set.

The phoneme specification method that we employ indicates feature contradiction associated with allophony in a strict binary-valued, fixed set of distinctive features through the introduction of special feature categories. Specifically, we utilize a small set of *corollary* features to mark the occasional, allophonic realizations of some primary features. A corollary feature is defined as a feature that supplements a primary feature in the system. The corollary features mark "occasionality" (associated with context dependency, dialectal variation, speech style variation, etc.) in the primary feature as either present or absent.

2.2 Primary and corollary features

Our feature set includes twenty-six primary articulatory features and six corollary features. The selected primary features conform to a typical set of hierarchically-related distinctive features (e.g. syllabic, sonorant, consonantal, labial, coronal, nasal, continuant, high, low, back, etc.) (Ladefoged 1975). In this hierarchical system, the presence of one feature presupposes the presence of those hierarchically dominant features. For example, the presence of the feature [alveolar] requires the presence of the feature [coronal], and the presence of the feature [nasal] requires the presence of the feature [sonorant]. Significantly, the reverse of these relations is not true. As is explained later in the next section, this feature structure allows for a linguistically-principled determination of feature salience in phonetic distance calculation.

Corollary features are restricted to specifying those primary features that are judged to be most significant to cross-language phoneme comparison *in an ASR environment*. Phoneme inventories designed for ASR comprise both phonemes and significant allophones, where a significant allophone is characteristically both acoustically distinct from the primary allophone and associated with a sufficiently high count of occurrence in the associated speech database. Thus American English ASR inventories regularly include an alveolar tap, a contextually-realized allophonic variant of both /t/ and /d/. Furthermore, pronunciation transcriptions in ASR lexica are typically phonetic - within the context of the phoneme-based inventory. So, word-final voice neutralization in German is overtly indicated throughout the lexicon (e.g. *hund* : h U n t). A typical ASR phoneme then does not represent a true phoneme; rather it encompasses only that phonemic variation that is not explicitly captured by its existing significant allophones in the inventory.

Corollary features specify variance that is not usually overtly indicated in ASR inventories and lexica but that is important to cross-language phoneme comparison in an acoustic, ASR environment. Internal phoneme recognition experiments indicate that generally major class features (syllabic, sonorant, etc.), manner features (nasal, continuant, etc.) and laryngeal features (voice, spread glottis, etc.) are more robustly identified than place features (labial, coronal, etc.); accordingly, the set of corollary features, provided in Table 1, predominantly targets particular major class, manner, and laryngeal features.

Table 1: Corollary features

Corollary Feature	Description
syllabic-occ	positive value marks the occasional realization of the phoneme as a syllabic consonant or glide
voice-occ	positive value marks the occasional voicing of phonemes
labial-occ	positive value marks the occasional rounding of vowels
nasal-occ	positive value marks the occasional nasalization of vowels and glides
rhotic-occ	positive value marks the occasional rhotization of liquids and vowels
spread-occ	positive value marks the occasional aspiration of obstruents

It should be pointed out that allophones that express a place contrast or difference in continuance with the primary realization of a phoneme are typically considered significant allophones in the ASR phoneme system and are therefore overtly represented.

As an illustration of the usefulness of corollary features in cross-language phoneme comparison, consider Table 2 which includes a partial feature matrix for the phoneme /k/ associated with 17 languages and dialects:

Table 2: Partial distinctive feature table

Languages	phoneme	spread glottis	spread -occ
Arabic	k	0	0
Danish	k	1	1
German	k	1	1
British English	k	1	1
U.S. English	k	1	1
Lat. Spanish	k	0	0
Can. French	k	0	0
Parisian French	k	0	0
Italian	k	0	0
Japanese	k	1	1
Dutch	k	0	0
Brz. Portuguese	k	0	0
Eur. Portuguese	k	0	0
Swedish	k	1	1
Korean	k	1	0
Cantonese	k	1	0
Mandarin	k	1	0

Note that the realization of the phoneme /k/ differs across the seventeen languages and dialects in the two features provided: [spread glottis] and [spread-occ]. The presence of the feature [spread glottis], marked by 1, and the non-presence of the corollary feature [spread-occ], marked by 0, indicates that the glottis is always open during the articulation of the phoneme; i.e. this phoneme is consistently associated with aspiration. The precise IPA transcription of this segment is /k^h/. A positive value for the corollary feature [spread-occ] means that the phoneme is only sometimes associated with aspiration. This phoneme has two principle phonetic realizations, marked [k] and [k^h] in IPA notation. A 0 value for the feature [spread glottis] and corollary feature [spread-occ] indicates that the segment is never aspirated. Thus this phoneme is most accurately labeled /k/ in IPA labeling.

Because this methodology incorporates phoneme feature contradiction, overall phonological similarity among languages and dialects is more precisely predicted:

Table 3: Phoneme similarity across languages

phoneme	allophone(s)	language	lang. family
k	k^h, k	Danish	Germanic
		German	Germanic
		Br. Eng.	Germanic
		Amer. Eng.	Germanic
		Japanese	Altaic
		Swedish	Germanic
	k^h	Korean	Altaic
		Mandarin	Sinitic
		Cantonese	Sinitic
	k	Arabic	Afro-Asiatic
		Lat. Span.	Romance
		Parisian Fr.	Romance
		Canadian Fr.	Romance
		Italian	Romance
		Dutch	Germanic
		Brz. Port.	Romance
		Eur. Port.	Romance

Table 3 reveals that Germanic languages tend to only occasionally aspirate /k/, Romance languages avoid aspirating /k/, and Sinitic languages typically aspirate /k/. Of course, closely related languages tend to be phonologically similar.

3 Phonetic distance

Most techniques for measuring phonetic distance between phonemes that do not assume speech data availability are based on articulatory features, though perceptual distance, judged (subjective) distance, and historical distance are also attested (Kessler 2005). We base our phonetic distance measurement on articulatory features because of their cross-linguistic consistency and general availability.

As Kessler notes, standard phonological theory provides no guidance in comparing phonetic distance between phonemes across multiple features (Kessler 2005). In our experiments to date, we use the Manhattan distance where the distance between phonemes equals the sum of the absolute values of individual feature distances. This approach is fairly standard in the literature, though the Euclidean distance has also been reported to attain good results (Kessler 2005).

Because features are known to differ in relative importance (Ladefoged 1969), some researchers apply weights or saliencies to the individual features for distance calculation. Nerbonne and Heeringa (1997), for example, weighted each feature by information gain, or entropy reduction. Kondrak (2002) expressed weights as coefficients that could be changed to any numeric value. He adjusted the coefficients until he achieved optimal performance on aligning cognate words.

In our approach, weights are derived from the lexica of all the considered languages. Specifically, the value of a weight for a feature is derived from the frequency of the feature in the lexica. Each language is treated equally in this approach; thus, the weights are not subject to the relative size of a language's lexicon.

Because our phoneme specification method incorporates hierarchical relations between features, feature weights are necessarily interdependent. Hierarchically dominant features are more frequently attested than their subordinate features and thus receive more weight. Further, hierarchically superior features tend to correspond to major phonetic categories (sonorant, consonantal, syllabic, etc.), which are expected to be more contrastive or distant to each other than sister subordinate categories. Thus, in a hierarchical feature system, lexical frequency of features is a reasonable indication of feature importance in phonetic contrast or distance.

In the following two subsections the phonetic distance algorithm is described.

Quantitative representation of phonemes

A phoneme is denoted by $p_l(i)$, where l (=1,...,L) represents the language that includes the phoneme, and i (=1,...,I_l) represents the index of the phoneme in language l. Thus, the phoneme inventory of language l is

(1) $\{p_l(i) \mid i = 1,\ldots,I_l\}$.

A phoneme $p_l(i)$ is represented by a vector of J features

(2) $\mathbf{f}[p_l(i)] = [v_l(i,j)]^T = [v_l(i,1),\ldots,v_l(i,j),\ldots,v_l(i,J)]^T$

where each $v_l(i,j)$ is a binary feature, $i = 1,\cdots,I_l$, $j = 1,\cdots,J$, $l = 1,\cdots,L$, and the superscript T denotes vector transposition.

Weighted phonetic distance

As mentioned, the value of a weight for a feature in the present phonetic distance approach is derived from the frequency of the feature in the lexica of all the considered languages. Let $c_l[p_l(i)]$ denote the occurrence count of a phoneme $p_l(i)$ in a lexicon of language l, then the frequency of each feature j contributed by the phoneme $p_l(i)$ is $c_l[p_l(i)]v_l(i,j)$, and the frequency of each feature j contributed by all the phonemes in language l is $\sum_{i=1}^{I_l} c_l[p_l(i)]v_l(i,j)$. The global weights derived from all the phonemes in all the languages are

(3) $\mathbf{W}(j) = diag\{w(1),\cdots,w(j),\cdots,w(J)\}$

where

(4)

$$w(j) = \frac{1}{L}\sum_{l=1}^{L} w_l(j) = \frac{1}{L}\sum_{l=1}^{L} \frac{\sum_{i=1}^{I_l} c_l[p_l(i)]v_l(i,j)}{\sum_{j=1}^{J}\sum_{i=1}^{I_l} c_l[p_l(i)]v_l(i,j)} \qquad j = 1,\cdots,J$$

where *diag*(vector) gives a diagonal matrix with elements of the vector as the diagonal entries. We define the phonetic distance between phonemes $p_l(i)$ and $p_t(k)$ in the form of a Manhattan distance, which is expressed as

(5)

$$d_{lt}(i,k) = \left\|\mathbf{W}(j)(\mathbf{f}[p_l(i)] - \mathbf{f}[p_t(k)])\right\|_1 = \sum_{j=1}^{J} w(j)\left|v_l(i,j) - v_t(k,j)\right|$$

where $i = 1,\cdots,I_l$, $k = 1,\cdots,I_t$, and the weights, given in a diagonal matrix $\mathbf{W}(j)$, are dependent upon the feature identity j.

4 Phonological distance metrics

Although our phoneme specification approach is designed to account for allophonic variance, not all variation is captured. Because of this, the effectiveness of measuring phonetic distance as a stand-alone strategy to predicting cross-language phoneme similarity is compromised. Furthermore, phonetic distance does not determine relative phoneme similarity in the not atypical scenario where two or more phonemes share the same phonetic distance to some target phoneme. In order to address these problems, phonological distance metrics are used to bias cross-language phoneme similarity predictions toward languages that have similar phoneme inventories and phoneme frequency distributions. The general idea is that the more similar the phoneme inventory and relative importance of each corresponding phoneme between languages, the more likely it is that the corresponding phonemes will be more similar.

Phonological distance consideration is especially desirable in an ASR environment because ultimately HMMs corresponding to those source-language phonemes predicted to be most similar to target-language phonemes must interact in a system that is intended to reflect a single target language. Use of phonological metrics then ensures that the overall model pool will have a bias toward a reduced set of phonologically similar languages, and it is reasonable to expect that similarity in languages of the model pool provides consistency in the target HMM system (see Schultz and Waibel 2000).

In this section, we define two distance metrics to characterize cross-language phonological similarity. One is based on monophoneme inventories while the other is based on biphoneme inventories.

4.1 Monophoneme distribution distance

Monophoneme distribution distance characterizes the difference in lexical phoneme distribution between two languages. Specifically, the distribution, or normalized histogram, of the phonemes is obtained from a large lexicon of a language, with the probability in the distribution corresponding to the frequency of a phoneme in the lexicon. We derive the distribution from a lexicon as we consider it more representative of a language's phonology than a particular database.

The monophoneme distribution metric is a typological comparison that is based on two principal classes of information: (1) types of sounds and (2) frequencies of these sounds in the lexicon. The former class is directly associated with phoneme inventory correspondence while the latter concerns relative phoneme importance.

Because the phoneme inventories of the two languages to be compared may not be identical, we first need to define a combined inventory for them

(6)

$$\{p_{lt}(m) \mid m = 1,\ldots,I_{lt}\} = \{p_l(i) \mid i = 1,\ldots,I_l\} \cup \{p_t(k) \mid k = 1,\ldots,I_t\}$$

where $p_{lt}(m)$ is a phoneme in the combined inventory where there are total I_{lt} phonemes.

The frequency of the phoneme $p_{lt}(m)$ in language l can be expressed as

(7) $$\rho_l[p_{lt}(m)] = \frac{c_l[p_{lt}(m)]}{\sum_{i=1}^{I_l} c_l[p_l(i)]}, \quad m = 1,\cdots,I_{lt}$$

where $c_l[p_{lt}(m)]$ is the occurrence count of phoneme $p_{lt}(m)$ in a lexicon of language l. If a phoneme $p_{lt}(m)$ does not exist in the language, its frequency would be zero. The difference of phoneme frequencies between the two languages can be calculated as

(8) $$d\rho_{lt}[p_{lt}(m)] = \left|\rho_l[p_{lt}(m)] - \rho_t[p_{lt}(m)]\right| \quad m = 1,\cdots,I_{lt}$$

Then the monophoneme distribution distance between the target language t and source language l is

(9) $$D\rho_{lt} = \sum_{m=1}^{I_{lt}} d\rho_{lt}[p_{lt}(m)] .$$

The distance is calculated between the target language and every one of the source languages.

In view of the known differences in phonological characteristics between vowels and consonants, we make separate calculations for the vowel and consonant categories. Thus Eq. (9) becomes

(10) $$D\rho_{lt}^{g} = \sum_{p_{lt}(m)\in g} d\rho_{lt}[p_{lt}(m)]$$

where g=Vowels or Consonants.

4.2 Biphoneme distribution distance

The biphoneme distribution distance metric characterizes the difference in lexical distribution of phoneme pairs, or biphonemes, between two languages. Similar to the monophoneme distribution distance, the distribution of biphonemes in a language is obtained based on the frequency of biphonemes in a large lexicon.

The biphoneme metric indicates how phonemes can combine in a language and how important these combinations are. Though the phonotactics provided in this approach is limited to only a sequence of two, the overall biphoneme inventory and distribution provides important phonological information. For example, it indicates if and to what extent consonants can cluster. Some languages tend to disfavor consonant clustering, like the Romance languages, while others allow for broad clustering, like the Germanic languages. It also indicates if and to what extent vowels may cooccur. Many languages require an onset consonant so vowels will never co-occur; other languages have no such restriction.

The biphoneme metric then yields types of information that are distinct from the monophoneme metric. It explicitly provides a biphoneme inventory, permissible phonotactic sequences, and phonotactic sequence importance. It also implicitly incorporates phoneme inventory and phonological complexity information.

Similar to the monophoneme distribution distance, the distribution of biphonemes in a language is obtained based on the frequency of a biphoneme in a large lexicon. The biphoneme inventory for the target language t is expressed as

(11) $\{q_t(k) \mid k = 1, \ldots, I'_t\}$

while the biphoneme inventory for a source language l is

(12) $\{q_l(i) \mid i = 1, \ldots, I'_l\}$

Then the combined biphoneme inventory for the two languages to be compared is

(13)

$$\{q_{lt}(n) \mid n = 1, \ldots, I'_{lt}\} = \{q_l(i) \mid i = 1, \ldots, I'_l\} \cup \{q_t(k) \mid k = 1, \ldots, I'_t\}$$

where $q_{lt}(n)$ is a biphoneme in the combined inventory where there are total I'_{lt} biphonemes. For a phoneme at the beginning or end of a word, $q_{lt}(n)$ takes the format of "void+phoneme" or "phoneme+void", respectively.

The frequency of a biphoneme $q_{lt}(n)$ in language l can be expressed as

(14) $$\gamma_l[q_{lt}(n)] = \frac{c_l[q_{lt}(n)]}{\sum_{i=1}^{I'_l} c_l[q_l(i)]}, \; n = 1, \cdots, I'_{lt}$$

where $c_l[q_{lt}(n)]$ is the occurrence count of biphoneme $q_{lt}(n)$ in a lexicon of language l. The difference of biphoneme frequencies between the two languages is

(15) $$d\gamma_{lt}[q_{lt}(n)] = \left|\gamma_l[q_{lt}(n)] - \gamma_t[q_{lt}(n)]\right| \quad n = 1, \cdots, I'_{lt}$$

Then the biphoneme distribution distance between the target language t and source language l is

(16) $$D\gamma_{lt} = \sum_{n=1}^{I'_{lt}} d\gamma_{lt}[q_{lt}(n)].$$

Similarly, the distance is better characterized within the categories of vowels and consonants separately. In our algorithm we count each biphoneme twice, the first time as a left-contact biphoneme and second time as a right-contact biphoneme. Thus

(17) $$D\gamma_{lt}^{g} = \sum_{\text{right of } q_{lt}(n) \in g} d\gamma_{lt}[q_{lt}(n)] + \sum_{\text{left of } q_{lt}(n) \in g} d\gamma_{lt}[q_{lt}(n)]$$

where g=Vowels or Consonants.

4.3 CPP phoneme distance

For phoneme similarity prediction, we unite the phonetic and phonological distance metrics to arrive at the CPP phoneme distance measurement. Since the three distances are from different domains and provide distinct types of information, normalization is necessary before combination. The normalization, aimed at extracting the relative ranking between source phonemes and languages, is a linear processing that scales the score range from each domain into the range [0 1].

We equate the overall importance of phonetics with that of phonology by providing a weight of 2 to the phonetic score and 1 to each of the phonological scores. By doing this, a source-language phoneme can have a greater phonetic distance to some target-language phoneme than other source-language phonemes but a lower phonological distance and receive a lower overall phoneme distance score. It is because phonological distance is considered as important as phonetic distance that the overall constructed target-language model pool will tend to be restricted to a subset of phonologically similar languages.

The feature-based phoneme distance metric is defined as

(18)

$$CPP(i,k) = \alpha_d \cdot [d_{lt}(i,k)]_N + \alpha_\rho \cdot [D\rho_{lt}^{g}]_N + \alpha_\gamma \cdot [D\gamma_{lt}^{g}]_N$$

where $CPP(i,k)$ represents the distance between phoneme $p_l(i)$ from language l and phoneme $p_t(k)$ from language t, and both phonemes belong to the same phonological category g (vowels or consonants). The weights α_d, α_ρ, and α_γ represent the relative importance of each quantity. As mentioned, ($\alpha_d, \alpha_\rho, \alpha_\gamma$)=(2,1,1). The symbol $[\cdot]_N$ denotes that the quantity inside is linearly scaled into the range [0 1]. For $D\rho_{lt}^{g}$ and $D\gamma_{lt}^{g}$, the original range is determined by scores of all the source languages. Their scaling is done once for a target language t. While for $d_{lt}(i,k)$, we found that it is better to do scaling once for each target phoneme $p_t(k)$, and the original range is determined by scores of a group of candidate phonemes that includes at least one phoneme from any source language.

5 Experiments

To test our CPP approach to phoneme similarity prediction, we compared it to an acoustic distance approach in ASR experiments. Because native language speech data is used in measuring model distance in the acoustic approach, it is expected to work better than the knowledge-based approach, which only estimates acoustic similarity indirectly through articulatory phonetic distance and overall phonological distance.

5.1 Model construction

We employ the regular 3-state, left-right, multimixture, continuous-Gaussian HMMs as the acoustic models and assume that the models from all the source and target languages have the same topology except that the number of mixtures in a state may vary. Once the top source phonemes are determined from our feature-based phoneme distance metric for each target phoneme, the target HMM is constructed by gathering all the mixtures for a corresponding state from the source candidates. The original mean and variance values are maintained while the mixture weights are uniformly scaled down so that the new weights add up to one for each state. It is possible to weigh mixtures according to the relative importance of the candidates if the importance as reflected by the phoneme distance metric has a significantly large difference. The transition probabilities are adopted from the top one candidate model.

5.2 CPP phoneme model construction

We used the 17 languages and dialects provided in Table 2 in the experiments testing our CPP phoneme distance approach to phoneme HMM similarity. For each language, a native monolingual model set had been built by training with native speech data. The acoustic features are 39 regular MFCC features including cepstral, delta, and delta-delta. The individual ASR databases derive from a variety of projects and protocols, including, but not limited to, CallHome, EUROM, SpeechDat, Polyphone, and GlobalPhone. In each of the following experiments, we select one language as the target language, and construct its acoustic models by using all the other languages as source languages. A phoneme distance score is calculated for each target phoneme and the top two candidate source-language phonemes are chosen for HMM model construction. We conducted experiments with Italian, Latin American Spanish, European Portuguese, Japanese, and Danish as target languages.

5.3 Acoustic model construction

In the acoustics distance approach, models are built with the top two models chosen from source languages based on their acoustic distance from the corresponding native target model. For these experiments, we adopt the widely used Bhattacharyya metric for the distance measurement (Mak and Barnard 1996). It should be noted that the recognition performance of the acoustics-constructed models is not a theoretically strict upper bound for HMM similarity because the measurement in the acoustic space is probabilistic.

5.4 Results

Each recognition task includes about 3000 utterances of digit strings, command words, and sentences. The word accuracy results in Table 4 include the native baseline performance, i.e. the performance of the native monolingual, context-independent models from each target language, as well as the acoustics-based and feature-based performances. These results show that the performance of models selected by the CPP phoneme distance approach is equivalent overall to that of models selected by acoustic distance.

Table 4: Model performance

Target Language	Native Baseline	Acoustic Distance	CPP Distance
Lat. Spanish	94.49	88.61	93.06
Italian	98.42	98.27	98.52
Japanese	95.36	76.72	78.76
Danish	94.36	72.95	70.15
Eur. Portuguese	96.31	77.91	72.74

The performance of models selected by the CPP approach nearly matches the performance of the *native* models for Latin American Spanish and surpasses those for Italian. This approach performs better than the acoustic distance approach for Latin American Spanish, Italian, and Japanese and not as well for Danish and European Portuguese.

6 Evaluation and conclusion

We suggest four principal performance factors to explain the results provided in Table 4: (1) rare phonemes in the target-language inventory; (2) target-language inventory complexity; (3) degree of source-language phonological distance to the target language; (4) reliability of source-language models. Because the CPP approach has only been tested on five languages, we consider this analysis preliminary.

Regarding the first factor, rare phonemes in the target-language inventory, it is worth noting that neither Latin American Spanish nor Italian has phonemes whose exact feature specifications are unattested in phonemes from other languages in our dataset. For these languages, all phonemes have exact source-language matches. In contrast, Japanese, Danish, and European Portuguese each contain phonemes with feature specifications unique to their language. Based on this analysis, we propose that, *all other factors being equal*, the greater the overall phoneme correspondence between the target language and the source languages, the better the target-language HMM performance.

In general, it appears that target languages associated with inventories that are greater in size than their least phonologically distant source languages perform worse than target languages associated with smaller inventories relative to their closest source languages. For example, the vowel systems of Danish, European Portuguese, and Japanese are the most complex of the five target languages, with Danish having 26 vowels, European Portuguese having 14 vowels, and Japanese having ten vowels. In sharp contrast, Latin American Spanish has only five vowels and Italian has seven. Both Latin American Spanish and Italian are phonologically similar to other Romance languages in the dataset that have greater vowel contrasts: Brazilian Portuguese (13 vowels), European Portuguese (14 vowels), Parisian French (17 vowels) and Canadian French (19 vowels). Here, we suggest that target languages that have a similar or lesser number of phoneme contrasts compared to the source languages are more likely to achieve higher recognition performances, *all other factors being equal.*

Relative phonological distance of the source languages to the target language and reliability of source language models additionally impact target-language ASR performance. Consider Table 5 where the difference in these factors for Italian and European Portuguese are given. First, Italian and European Portuguese are both Romance languages and our dataset includes a total of six, presumably phonologically similar, Romance languages and dialects. However, the recognition results of the models selected by both the feature-based and acoustics-based phoneme distance method are very different for the two languages.

Table 5: Phonological distance and native baseline performance factors in target-language recognition

Target Language	Italian	Eur. Portuguese
Top 3 least distant langs.	(1) Lat. Spanish (2) Parisian Fr. (3) Brz. Port.	(1) Brz. Port. (2) Lat. Spanish (3) Canadian Fr.
Avg. phonolog. distance of top 3 langs.	0.7399	0.8945
Avg. phonolog. distance of top 1 lang.	0.5757	0.8248
Avg. native baseline of top 3 langs.	89	91.94
Native baseline of top 1 lang.	94.49	84.25

If we compare the phonological distances between the least distant source languages to Italian and European Portuguese, we observe that Italian's closest languages are less distant overall than European Portuguese's closest languages.

Because the phonologically least distant source languages contribute the majority of target-language HMMs, it is reasonable to expect that lesser phonological distance to the target language by a greater number of source languages is likely to result in a better target-language HMM performance, *all other factors being equal.*

Finally, note the substantial discrepancy in native baseline performance between the phonologically least distant source languages for Italian and European Portuguese. The majority of selected models for Italian derive from Latin American Spanish which is associated with a high native recognition baseline. European Portuguese models, on the other hand, largely come from Brazilian Portuguese which has a much lower native baseline. This suggests that the most reliable source-language HMMs, as judged from their native recognition performance, contribute to better target-language recognition performance, *all other factors being equal.*

In future work, we intend to test our CPP phoneme similarity approach on new target languages and expand the preliminary evaluation provided here. In particular, we are interested to what extent this method can predict recognition performance for new target languages.

References

Archangeli, D., "Aspects of Underspecification Theory". *Phonology* 5:183-207, 1988.

Connolly, J. H., "Quantifying target-realization differences," *Clinical Linguistics & Phonetics*, 11:267–298, 1997.

IPA, *Handbook of the International Phonetic Association*, Oxford University Press, 1999.

Kessler, B., "Computational dialectology in Irish Gaelic," *Proc. 6th Conf. European Chapter of ACL*, 60–67, 1995.

Kessler, B., "Phonetic comparison algorithms," *Transactions of the Philological Society*, 2005

Köhler J., "Multilingual phoneme recognition exploiting acoustic-phonetic similarities of sounds," *ICSLP'96*, 2195-2198, Philadelphia, 1996.

Kondrak, G., *Algorithms for Language Reconstruction*, Ph.D. thesis, University of Toronto, 2002.

Ladefoged P., "The measurement of phonetic similarity," *Int Conf on Comp Linguistics*, Stockholm, Sweden, 1969.

Ladefoged P. *A Course in Phonetics*. Harcourt Brace Jovanovich, New York, 1975.

Liu, C. and Melnar, L., "An automated linguistic knowledge-based cross-language transfer method for building acoustic models for a language without native training data," *Interspeech'05*, 1365-1368, Lisbon, 2005.

Liu, C. and Melnar, L., "Training acoustic models with speech data from different languages," *MULTILING'06*, Stellenbosch, 2006.

Mak, B. and Barnard, E., "Phone clustering using the Bhattacharyya distance," *ICSLP'96*, 2005-2008, 1996.

Nerbonne, J. and Heeringa, W., "Measuring dialect distance phonetically," *Proc. 3rd Meeting ACL Special Interest Group in Comp. Phonology*, 1997.

Schultz, T. and Waibel, A., "Fast bootstrapping of LVCSR systems with multilingual phoneme sets," *Eurospeech 97*, 1:371-373, 1997.

Schultz, T. and Waibel, A.., "Polyphone Decision Tree Specialization for Language Adaptation", In *Proc. of ICASSP 2000*. Istanbul, 2000.

Somers, H. L., "Similarity metrics for aligning children's articulation data," *Proc. 36th Annual Meeting ACL and 17th Int. Conf. Comp. Ling.*, 1227–1231, 1998.

Sooful, J. J. and Botha, E. C., "Comparison of acoustic distance measures for automatic cross-language phoneme mapping," *ICSLP'02*, 521-524, 2002.

Improving Syllabification Models with Phonotactic Knowledge

Karin Müller
Institute of Phonetic Sciences
University of Amsterdam
kmueller@science.uva.nl

Abstract

We report on a series of experiments with probabilistic context-free grammars predicting English and German syllable structure. The treebank-trained grammars are evaluated on a syllabification task. The grammar used by Müller (2002) serves as point of comparison. As she evaluates the grammar only for German, we re-implement the grammar and experiment with additional phonotactic features. Using bi-grams within the syllable, we can model the dependency from the previous consonant in the onset and coda. A 10-fold cross validation procedure shows that syllabification can be improved by incorporating this type of phonotactic knowledge. Compared to the grammar of Müller (2002), syllable boundary accuracy increases from 95.8% to 97.2% for English, and from 95.9% to 97.2% for German. Moreover, our experiments with different syllable structures point out that there are dependencies between the onset on the nucleus for German but not for English. The analysis of one of our phonotactic grammars shows that interesting phonotactic constraints are learned. For instance, unvoiced consonants are the most likely first consonants and liquids and glides are preferred as second consonants in two-consonantal onsets.

1 Introduction

In language technology applications, unknown words are a continuous problem. Especially, Text-to-speech (TTS) systems like those described in Sproat (1998) depend on the correct pronunciation of those words. Most of these systems use large pronunciation dictionaries to overcome this problem. However, the lexicons are finite and every natural language has productive word formation processes. Thus, a TTS system needs a module which converts letters to sounds and a second module which syllabifies these sound sequences. The syllabification information is important to assign the stress status of the syllable, to calculate the phone duration (Van Santen et al. (1997)), and to apply phonological rules (Kahn (1976), Blevins (1995)). Many automatic syllabification methods have been suggested e.g., (Daelemans and van den Bosch, 1992; Van den Bosch, 1997; Kiraz and Möbius, 1998; Vroomen et al., 1998; Müller, 2001; Marchand et al., to appear 2006). Müller (2001) shows that incorporating syllable structure improves the prediction of syllable boundaries. The syllabification accuracy increases if the onset and coda is more fine-grained (Müller, 2002). However, she only incorporates partial phonotactic knowledge in her approach. For instance, her models cannot express that the phoneme /l/ is more likely to occur after an /s/ than after a /t/ in English. The information that a phoneme is very probable in a certain position (here, the /l/ appears as second consonant in a two-consonantal onset cluster) will not suffice to express English phonotactics of an entire consonant cluster. Moreover, she

Proceedings of the Eighth Meeting of the ACL Special Interest Group on Computational Phonology at HLT-NAACL 2006, pages 11–20,
New York City, USA, June 2006.

only reports the performance of the German grammar. Thus, we are interested if the detection of syllable boundaries can be improved for both English and German by adding further phonotactic knowledge to a grammar.

Phonotactic constraints within the onset or coda seem to be important for various tasks. Listeners indeed use phonotactic knowledge from their mother language in various listening situations. Vitevitch and Luce (1999), e.g., showed if English speakers have to rate nonsense words how "English-like" the stimuli are, highly probable phonotactic stimuli were rated more "English-like" than stimuli with a lower probability. Speakers make also use of their phonotactic knowledge when they have to segment a sequence into words. In a words spotting task, Weber and Cutler (2006) found evidence that speakers of American English can segment words much easier when the sequence contains phonotactic constraints of their own language.

Beside many perception experiments which show that phonotactic constraints are useful information, many different methods have been suggested to model phonotactic constraints for language technology applications. Krenn (1997), for instance, uses Hidden Markov Models to tag syllable structure. The model decides whether a phoneme belongs to the onset, nucleus or coda. However, this model does not incorporate fine-grained phonotactics. Belz (2000) uses finite state automatons (FSA) to model phonotactic structure of different syllable types. We use similar positional features of syllables. Moreover, Carson-Berndsen (1998) and Carson-Berndsen et al. (2004) focus on automatically acquiring feature-based phonotactics by induction of automata which can be used in speech recognition. In our approach, we concentrate on explicit phonotactic grammars as we want to test different suggestions about the internal structure of words from phonological approaches (e.g. Kessler and Treiman (1997)). We assume, for instance, that codas depend on the previous nucleus and that onsets depend on the subsequent nucleus.

In this paper, we present experiments on a series of context-free grammars which integrate step by step more phonological structure. The paper is organized as follows: we first introduce our grammar development approach. In section 3, we describe our experiments and the evaluation procedure. The subsequent section 4 shows what kind of phonotactic information can be learned from a phonotactic grammar. Last, we discuss our results and draw some conclusions.

2 Method

We build on the approach of Müller (2001) which combines the advantages of treebank and bracketed corpora training. Her method consists of four steps: (i) writing a (symbolic i.e. non-probabilistic) context-free phonological grammar with syllable boundaries, (ii) training this grammar on a pronunciation dictionary which contains markers for syllable boundaries (see Example 1; the pre-terminals "X[" and "X]" denote the beginning and end of a syllable such that syllables like [strIN] can be unambiguously processed during training), (iii) transforming the resulting probabilistic phonological grammar by dropping the syllable boundary markers[1] (see Example 2), and (iv) predicting syllable boundaries of unseen phoneme strings by choosing their most probable phonological tree according to the transformed probabilistic grammar. The syllable boundaries can be extracted from the *Syl* node which governs a whole syllable.

(1) Word $\rightarrow$ X[Syl_{one}]X
(2) Word $\rightarrow$ Syl_{one}

We use a grammar development procedure to describe the phonological structure of words. We expect that a more fine-grained grammar increases the precision of the prediction of syllable boundaries as more phonotactic information can be learned. In the following section, we describe the development of a series of grammars.

2.1 Grammar development

Our point of comparison is (i) the *syllable complexity grammar* which was introduced by Müller (2002). We develop four different grammars: (ii) the *phonotactic grammar*, (iii) the *phonotactic on-nuc grammar* (iv) the *phonotactic nuc-coda grammar* and (v) the *phonotactic on-nuc-coda grammar*. All five grammars share the following features: The grammars describe a word which is composed of one

[1] We also drop rules with zero probabilities

to n syllables which in turn branch into onset and rhyme. The rhyme is re-written by the nucleus and the coda. Onset or coda could be empty. Furthermore, all grammar versions differentiate between monosyllabic and polysyllabic words. In polysyllabic words, the syllables are divided into syllables appearing word-initially, word-medially, and word-finally. Additionally, the grammars distinguish between consonant clusters of different sizes (ranging from one to five consonants).

We assume that phonotactic knowledge within the onset and coda can help to solve a syllabification task. Hence, we change the rules of the *syllable complexity grammar* (Müller, 2002) such that phonotactic dependencies are modeled. We express the dependencies within the onset and coda as well as the dependency from the nucleus by bi-grams.

2.1.1 Grammar generation

The grammars are generated automatically (using perl-scripts). As all possible phonemes in a language are known, our grammar generates all possible re-write rules. This generation process naturally over-generates, which means that we receive rules which will never occur in a language. There are, for instance, rules which describe the impossible English onset /tRS/. However, our training procedure and our training data make sure that only those rules will be chosen which occur in a certain language.

The monosyllabic English word *string* is used as a running example to demonstrate the differences of the grammar versions. The word *string* is transcribed in the pronunciation dictionary CELEX as ([strIN]) (Baayen et al., 1993). The opening square bracket, "[", indicates the beginning of the syllable and the closing bracket, "]", the end of the syllable. The word consists of the tri-consonantal onset $[str]$ followed by the nucleus, the short vowel $[I]$ and the coda $[N]$.

In the following paragraphs, we will introduce the different grammar versions. For comparison reasons, we briefly describe the grammar of Müller (2002) first.

2.1.2 Syllable complexity grammar (Müller, 2002)

The syllable complexity grammar distinguishes between onsets and codas which contain a different number of consonants. There are different rules which describe zero to n-consonantal onsets. Tree (3) shows the complete analysis of the word *string*.

(3)

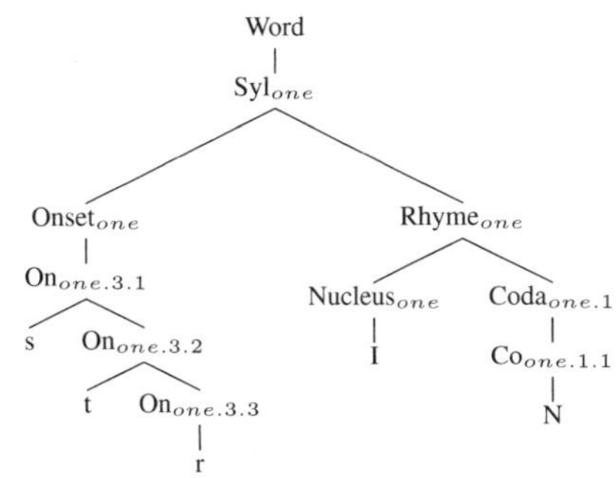

(4) $\text{On}_{one.3.1} \rightarrow \text{s} \quad \text{On}_{one.3.2}$

(5) $\text{On}_{one.2.1} \rightarrow \text{s} \quad \text{On}_{one.2.2}$

Rule 4, e.g., describes a tri-consonantal onset, e.g., $[str]$. This rule occurs in example tree 3 and will be used for words such as ***string*** or ***spray***. Rule (5) describes a two-consonantal onset occurring in the analysis of words such as ***snake*** or ***stand***. However, this grammar cannot model phonotactic dependencies from the previous consonant.

2.1.3 Phonotactic grammar

Thus, we develop a phonotactic grammar which differs from the previous one. Now, a consonant in the onset or coda depends on the preceding one. The rules express bi-grams of the onset and coda consonants. The main difference to the previous grammars can be seen in the re-writing rules involving phonemic preterminal nodes (rule 6) as well as terminal nodes for consonants (rule 7).

(6) $\mathbf{X}\text{.r.C.s.t} \rightarrow \text{C} \quad \mathbf{X}\text{.r.C}^{+}\text{.s.t}$

(7) $\mathbf{X}\text{.r.C.s.t} \rightarrow \text{C}$

Rules of this type bear four features for a consonant C inside an onset or a coda (**X**=On, Cod), namely: the position of the syllable in the word (r=ini, med, fin, one), the current terminal node ($C = consonant$), the succeeding consonant (C^{+}), the cluster size ($t = 1 \dots 5$), and the position of a consonant within a cluster ($s = 1 \dots 5$).

The example tree (8) shows the analysis of the word *string* with the current grammar version. The rule (9) comes from the example tree showing that the onset consonant $[t]$ depends on the previous consonant $[s]$.

(8)

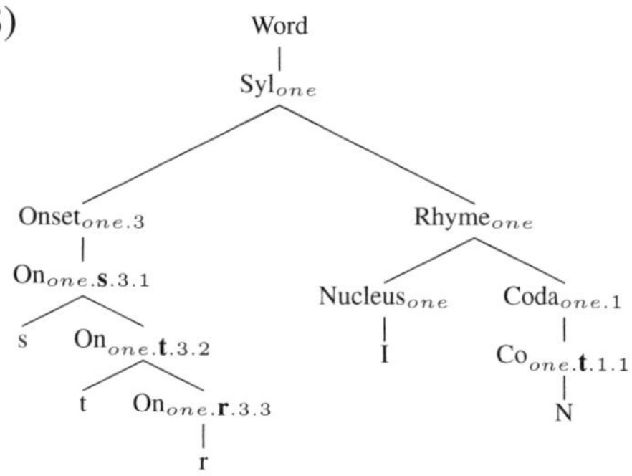

(9) $\text{On}_{one.s.3.1} \rightarrow \quad \text{s} \quad \text{On}_{one.t.3.2}$

2.1.4 Phonotactic on-nuc grammar

We also examine if there are dependencies of the first onset consonant on the succeeding nucleus. The dependency of the whole onset on the nucleus is indirectly encoded by the bi-grams within the onset. The phonotactic onset-nucleus grammar distinguishes between same onsets with different nuclei. In example tree (12), the triconsonantal onset starting with a phoneme $[s]$ depends on the Nucleus $[I]$. Rule (10) occurs in tree (12) and will be also used for words such as *strict* or *strip* whereas rule (11) is used for words such as *strong* or *strop*.

(10) $\text{Onset}_{one.\mathbf{I}.3} \rightarrow \text{On}_{one.s.3.1}$
(11) $\text{Onset}_{one.\mathbf{O}.3} \rightarrow \text{On}_{one.s.3.1}$
(12)

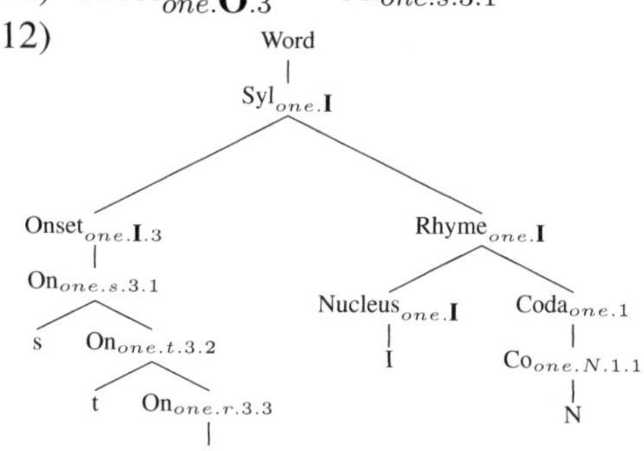

2.1.5 Phonotactic nuc-coda grammar

The phonotactic nucleus-coda grammar encodes the dependency of the first coda consonant on the nucleus. The grammar distinguishes between codas that occur with various nuclei. Rule 13 is used, for instance, to analyze the word *string*, shown in Example tree 15. The same rule will be applied for words such as *bring, king, ring* or *thing*. If there is a different nucleus, we get a different set of rules. Rule 14, e.g., is required to analyze words such as *long, song, strong* or *gong*.

(13) $\text{Coda}_{one.\mathbf{I}.1} \rightarrow \quad \text{N Co}_{one.t.1.1}$
(14) $\text{Coda}_{one.\mathbf{O}.1} \rightarrow \quad \text{N Co}_{one.t.1.1}$
(15)

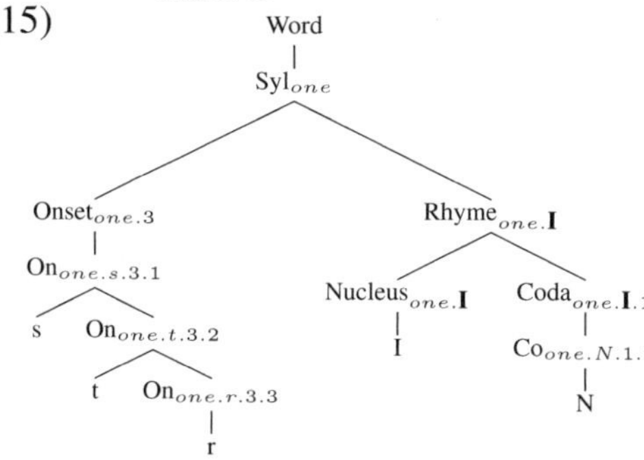

2.1.6 Phonotactic on-nuc-coda grammar

The last tested grammar is the phonotactic onset-nucleus-coda grammar. It is a combination of grammar 2.1.4 and 2.1.5. In this grammar, the first consonant of the onset and coda depend on the nucleus. Tree 16 shows the full analysis of our running example word *string*.

(16)

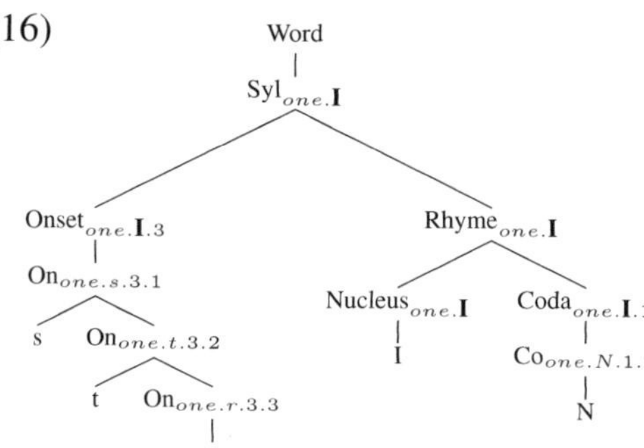

The rules of the subtree (17) are the same for words such as *string* or *spring*. However, words with a different nucleus such as *strong* will be analyzed with a different set of rules.

(17)

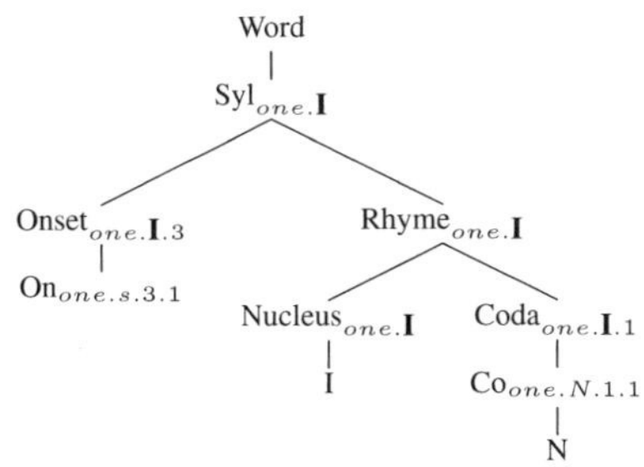

3 Experiments

In this section, we report on our experiments with four different phonotactic grammars introduced in Section 2.1 (see grammar 2.1.3-2.1.6), as well as with a re-implementation of Müller's less complex grammar (Müller, 2002). All these grammars are trained on a corpus of transcribed words from the pronunciation lexicon CELEX. We use the full forms of the lexicon instead of the lemmas. The German lexicon contains 304,928 words and the English lexicon 71,493 words. Homographs with the same pronunciation but with different part of speech tags are taken only once. We use for our German experiments 274,435 words for training and 30,492 for testing (evaluating). For our English experiments, we use 64,343 for training and 7,249 for testing.

3.1 Training procedure

We use the same training procedure as Müller (2001). It is a kind of treebank training where we obtain a probabilistic context-free grammar (PCFG) by observing how often each rule was used in the training corpus. The brackets of the input guarantee an unambiguous analysis of each word. Thus, the formula of treebank training given by (Charniak, 1996) is applied: r is a rule, let $|r|$ be the number of times r occurred in the parsed corpus and $\lambda(r)$ be the non-terminal that r expands, then the probability assigned to r is given by

$$p(r) = \frac{|r|}{\sum_{r' \in \{r' | \lambda(r') = \lambda(r)\}} |r'|}$$

After training, we transform the PCFG by dropping the brackets in the rules resulting in an analysis grammar. The bracket-less analysis grammar is used for parsing the input without brackets; i.e., the phoneme strings are parsed and the syllable boundaries are extracted from the most probable parse.

In our experiments, we use the same technique. The advantage of this training method is that we learn the distribution of the grammar which maximizes the likelihood of the corpus.

3.2 Evaluation procedure

We evaluate our grammars on a syllabification task which means that we use the trained grammars to predict the syllable boundaries of an unseen corpus. As we drop the explicit markers for syllable boundaries, the grammar can be used to predict the boundaries of arbitrary phoneme sequences. The boundaries can be extracted from the *syl*-span which governs an entire syllable.

Our training and evaluation procedure is a 10-fold cross validation procedure. We divide the original (German/English) corpus into ten parts equal in size. We start the procedure by training on parts 1-9 and evaluating on part 10. In a next step, we take parts 1-8 and 10 and evaluate on part 9. Then, we evaluate on corpus 8 and so forth. In the end, this procedure yields evaluation results for all 10 parts of the original corpus. Finally, we calculate the average mean of all evaluation results.

3.2.1 Evaluation Metrics

Our three evaluation measures are word accuracy, syllable accuracy and syllable boundary accuracy. Word accuracy is a very strict measure and does not depend on the number of syllables within a word. If a word is correctly analyzed the accuracy increases. We define **word accuracy** as

$$\frac{\#\ of\ correctly\ analyzed\ words}{total\ \#\ of\ words}$$

Syllable accuracy is defined as

$$\frac{\#\ of\ correctly\ analyzed\ syllables}{total\ \#\ of\ syllables}$$

The last evaluation metrics we used is the **syllable boundary accuracy**. It expresses how reliable the boundaries were recognized. It is defined as

$$\frac{\#\ of\ correctly\ analyzed\ syllable\ boundaries}{total\ \#\ of\ syllable\ boundaries}$$

The difference between the three metrics can be seen in the following example. Let our evaluation corpus consist of two words, *transferring* and *wet*. The transcription and the syllable boundaries are displayed in table 1. Let our trained grammar predict the boundaries shown in table 2. Then the word accuracy will be 50%

transferring	trA:ns–f3:–rIN
wet	wEt

Table 1: Example: evaluation corpus

transferring	trA:n–sf3:–rIN
wet	wEt

Table 2: Example: predicted boundaries

($\frac{1\ correct\ word}{2\ words}$), the syllable accuracy will be 50% ($\frac{2\ correct\ syllables}{4\ syllables}$), and the syllable boundary accuracy is 75% ($\frac{3\ correct\ syllable\ boundaries}{4\ syllable\ boundaries}$). The difference between syllable accuracy and syllable boundary accuracy is that the first metric punishes the wrong prediction of a syllable boundary twice as the complete syllable has to be correct. The syllable boundary accuracy only judges the end of the syllable and counts how often it is correct. Mono-syllabic words are also included in this measure. They serve as a baseline as the syllable boundary will be always correct. If we compare the baseline for English and German (tables 3 and 4, respectively), we observe that the English dictionary contains 10.3% monosyllabic words and the German one 1.59%.

Table 3 and table 4 show that phonotactic knowledge improves the prediction of syllable boundaries. The syllable boundary accuracy increases from 95.84% to 97.15% for English and from 95.9% to 96.48% for German. One difference between the two languages is if we encode the nucleus in the onset or coda rules, German can profit from this information compared to English. This might point at a dependence of German onsets from the nucleus. For English, it is even the case that the on-nuc and the nuc-cod grammars worsen the results compared to the phonotactic base grammar. Only the combination of the two grammars (the on-nuc-coda grammar) achieves a higher accuracy than the phonotactic grammar. We suspect that the on-nuc-coda grammar encodes that onset and coda constrain each other on the repetition of liquids or nasals between /s/C onsets and codas. For instance, *lull* and *mam* are okey, whereas *slull* and *smame* are less good.

4 Learning phonotactics from PCFGs

We want to demonstrate in this section that our phonotactic grammars does not only improve syllabification accuracy but can be used to reveal interesting phonotactic[2] information at the same time. Our intension is to show that it is possible to augment symbolic studies such as e.g., Hall (1992), Pierrehumbert (1994), Wiese (1996), Kessler and Treiman (1997), or Ewen and van der Hulst (2001) with extensive probabilistic information. Due to time and place constraints, we concentrate on two-consonantal clusters of grammar 2.1.3.

grammar version	word accuracy	syllable accuracy	syll bound. accuracy
baseline	10.33%		
(Müller, 2002)	89.27%	91.84%	95.84%
phonot. grammar	92.48%	94.35%	97.15%
phonot. on-nuc	92.29%	94.21%	97.09%
phonot. nuc-cod	92.39%	94.27%	97.11%
phonot. on-nuc-cod	92.64%	94.47%	**97.22%**

Table 3: Evaluation of four English grammar versions.

grammar version	word accuracy	syllable accuracy	syll bound. accuracy
baseline	1.59%		
(Müller, 2002)	86.06%	91.96%	95.90%
phonot. grammar	87.95%	93.09%	96.48%
phonot. nuc-cod	89.53%	94.09%	97.01%
phonot. on-nuc	89.97%	94.35%	97.15%
phonot. on-nuc-cod	90.45%	94.62%	**97.29%**

Table 4: Evaluation of four German grammar versions.

Phonotactic restrictions are often expressed by tables which describe the possibility of combination of consonants. Table 5 shows the possible combinations of German two-consonantal onsets (Wiese, 1996). However, the table cannot express differences in frequency of occurrence between certain clusters. For instance, it does not distinguish between onset clusters such as [pfl] and [kl]. If we consider the frequency of occurrence in a German dictionary then there is indeed a great difference. [kl] is much more common than [pfl].

4.1 German

Our method allows additional information to be added to tables such as shown in table 5. In what follows, the probabilities are taken from the rules of grammar 2.1.3. Table 6 shows the probability of

[2]Note that we only deal with phonotactic phenomena on the syllable level and not on the morpheme level.

mono		l	R	n	m	s	v	f	t	ts	p	k	j	z	g
0.380	S	0.160	0.093	0.056	0.074		0.165		0.318		0.131				
0.158	k	0.351	0.322	0.175			0.151								
0.090	b	0.489	0.510												
0.086	t		0.955				0.044								
0.083	f	0.620	0.364										0.015		
0.066	g	0.362	0.617	0.019											
0.042	p	0.507	0.400	0.030		0.061									
0.033	d		1.000												
0.019	s	0.200		0.066	0.100		0.133	0.033			0.133	0.333			
0.019	ts						1.000								
0.011	pf	0.882	0.117												
0.007	v		1.000												

Table 6: German two-consonantal onsets in monosyllabic words - sorted by probability of occurrence

mono		l	r	n	m	s	v	f	t	ts	p	k	j	z	g	w	S	d
0.322	s	0.157	0.001	0.099	0.060		0.001	0.004	0.223		0.150	0.174	0.006			0.120		
0.148	k	0.375	0.390		0.003		0.003						0.030			0.196		
0.093	b	0.420	0.574										0.004					
0.083	f	0.591	0.333										0.075					
0.079	p	0.480	0.457										0.056				0.005	
0.072	g	0.283	0.709													0.006		
0.068	t		0.686										0.039			0.274		
0.048	d		0.822										0.112			0.065		
0.035	h												0.089			0.910		
0.018	T		0.857										0.047			0.095		
0.014	S		0.878	0.030	0.030											0.060		
0.004	m												1.000					
0.003	n												1.000					
0.002	l												1.000					
0.002	v												1.000					

Table 7: English two-consonantal onsets in monosyllabic words - sorted by probability of occurrence

	Sonorants				Obstruents	
	l	R	n	m	s	v
Obstruents						
p	+	+	(+)	-	+	-
t	-	+	-	-	-	(+)
k	+	+	+	(+)	(+)	+
b	+	+	-	-	-	-
d	-	+	-	-	-	-
g	+	+	+	(+)	-	-
f	+	+	-	-	-	-
v	(+)	+	-	-	-	
ts	-	-	-	-	-	+
pf	+	+	-	-	-	-
S	+	+	+	+	-	+

Table 5: (Wiese, 1996) German onset clusters

occurrence of German obstruents ordered by their probability of occurrence. [S] occurs very often in German words as first consonant in two-consonantal onsets word initially. In the first row of table 6, the consonants which occur as second consonants are listed. We observe, for instance, that [St] is the most common two-consonantal onset in monosyllabic words. This consonant cluster appears in words such as *Staub* (dust), *stark* (strong), or *Stolz* (pride). We believe that there is a threshold indicating that a certain combination is very likely to come from a loanword. If we define the probability of a two-consonantal onset as

$$p(onset\_ini\_2) =_{def} p(C_1) \times p(C_2)$$

where $p(C_1)$ is the probability of the rule

$$\mathbf{X}.\text{r.C}_1.\text{s.t} \rightarrow \text{C}_1 \;\; \mathbf{X}.\text{r.C}_2.\text{s.t}$$

and $p(C_2)$ is the probability of the rule

$$\mathbf{X}.\text{r.C}_2.\text{s.t} \rightarrow \text{C}_2,$$

then we get a list of two-consonantal onsets ordered by their probabilities:

$$p(St) > ... > p(sk) > p(pfl) > p(sl) > ... > p(sf)$$

These onsets occur in words such as *Steg* (footbridge), *stolz* (proud), *Staat* (state), *Skalp* (scalp), *Skat* (skat) *Pflicht* (duty), *Pflock* (stake), or *Slang* (slang) and *Slum* (slum). The least probable combination is [sf] which appears in the German word *Sphäre* (sphere) coming from the Latin word *sphaera*. The consonant cluster [sl] is also a very uncommon onset. Words with this onset are usually loanwords from English. The onset [sk], however, is an onset which occur more often in German words. Most of the words are originally from Latin and are translated into German long ago. Interestingly, the onset [pfl] is also a very uncommon onset. Most of these onsets result from the second sound shift where in certain positions the simple onset consonant /p/ became the affricate /pf/. The English translation of these words shows that the second sound shift was not applied to English. However, the most probable two-consonantal onset is [St]. The whole set of two-consonantal onsets can be seen in Table 8.

4.2 English

English two-consonantal onsets show that unvoiced first consonants are more common than voiced ones. However, two combinations are missing. The alveolar plosives /t/ and /d/ do not combine with the lateral /l/ in English two-consonantal onsets. Table 8 shows the most probable two-consonantal onsets sorted by their joint probability.

4.3 Comparison between English and German

The fricatives /s/ and /S/ are often regarded as extra syllabic. According to our study on two-consonantal onsets, these fricatives are very probable first consonants and combine with more second consonants than all other first consonants. They seem to form an own class. Liquids and glides are the most important second consonants. However, English prefers /r/ over /l/ in all syllable positions and /j/ over /w/ (except in monosyllabic words) and /n/ as second consonants. Nasals can only combine with very little first consonants. In German, we observe that /R/ is preferred over /l/ and /v/ over /n/ and /j/. Moreover, the nasal /n/ is much more common in German than in English as second consonants which applies especially to medial and final syllables.

When we compare the phonotactic restrictions of two languages, it is also interesting to observe which combinations are missing. If certain consonant clusters are not very likely or never occur in a language, this might have consequences for language understanding and language learning. Phonotactic gaps in one language might cause spelling mistakes in a second language. For instance, a typical Northern German name is *Detlef* which is often misspelled in English as *Deltef*. The onset cluster /tl/ can occur in medial and final German syllables but not in English. The different phonetic realization of /l/ may play a certain role that /lt/ is more natural than /tl/ in English.

Mono-syllabic: /st/ > /kr/ > /sk/ > /kl/ > /br/ > /gr/ > /sl/ > /fl/ > /sp/ > /tr/ > /dr/ > /bl/ > /sw/ > /pl/ > /pr/ > /sn/ > /hw/ > /kw/ > /fr/ > /gl/ > /sm/ > /tw/ > /Tr/ > /Sr/ > /fj/ > /dj/ > /kj/ > /pj/ > /mj/ > /dw/ > /hj/ > /nj/ > /tj/ > /vj/ > /lj/ > /sj/ > /Tw/ > /sf/ > /Tj/ > /Sw/ > /km/ > /kv/ > /gw/ > /Sn/ > /Sm/ > /pS/ > /bj/ > /sr/ > /sv/
Initial /pr/ > /st/ > /tr/ > /kr/ > /sp/ > /sk/ > /br/ > /gr/ > /fl/ > /kl/ > /fr/ > /bl/ > /pl/ > /sl/ > /kw/ > /dr/ > /sn/ > /sw/ > /gl/ > /hw/ > /nj/ > /sm/ > /sj/ > /pj/ > /Tr/ > /mj/ > /kj/ > /dj/ > /tw/ > /tj/ > /fj/ > /hj/ > /lj/ > /bj/ > /ps/ > /Sr/ > /dw/ > /sf/ > /vj/ > /gj/ > /gw/ > /pw/ > /mn/ > /Sm/ > /Tj/ > /Tw/ > /Sn/ > /tsw/ > /zj/ > /pt/ > /mw/ > /kn/ > /gz/
Medial: /st/ > /tr/ > /pr/ > /sp/ > /gr/ > /kj/ > /kr/ > /kw/ > /pl/ > /br/ > /tj/ > /lj/ > /dj/ > /dr/ > /kl/ > /nj/ > /sk/ > /mj/ > /fr/ > /pj/ > /bl/ > /fl/ > /bj/ > /gl/ > /gj/ > /fj/ > /Sn/ > /sj/ > /vj/ > /Sj/ > /Tr/ > /vr/ > /gw/ > /sl/ > /nr/ > /sw/ > /mr/ > /sn/ > /hj/ > /hw/ > /sm/ > /zj/ > /tSr/ > /rj/ > /sr/ > /dw/ > /Zr/ > /Sr/ > /jw/ > /tSw/ > /tSn/ > /vw/ > /Dr/ > /dZr/ > /dn/ > /Tj/ > /tw/ > /Sw/ > /Zj/ > /zr/ > /zn/ > /zw/ > /Zw/ > /dZj/ > /dZn/ > /dZw/
Final: /st/ > /tr/ > /kl/ > /bl/ > /gr/ > /dr/ > /pl/ > /br/ > /sk/ > /sp/ > /pr/ > /kr/ > /tj/ > /fr/ > /nj/ > /fl/ > /lj/ > /kw/ > /dj/ > /sj/ > /kj/ > /sl/ > /gl/ > /hw/ > /Sn/ > /vr/ > /Sj/ > /vj/ > /bj/ > /pj/ > /fj/ > /Tr/ > /mj/ > /gw/ > /sr/ > /sw/ > /sm/ > /nr/ > /sn/ > /tSr/ > /mr/ > /tw/ > /dZr/ > /zj/ > /gj/ > /dZj/ > /Sr/ > /Zr/ > /sf/ > /nw/ > /zr/ > /Tj/ > /rj/ > /Dr/ > /vw/ > /dw/ > /dn/ > /tSj/ > /pw/ > /jw/ > /hj/ > /St/ > /Zw/ > /tSn/ > /Zj/ > /pn/ > /Dj/ > /dZn/ > /zn/ > /Sw/ > /Zn/ > /tSw/ > /Tw/ > /bd/ > /tsj/ > /Dw/

Monosyllabic: /St/ > /tR/ > /Sv/ > /Sl/ > /kl/ > /fl/ > /kR/ > /Sp/ > /bR/ > /bl/ > /gR/ > /SR/ > /dR/ > /fR/ > /Sm/ > /kn/ > /gl/ > /kv/ > /pl/ > /Sn/ > /tsv/ > /pR/ > /pfl/ > /vR/ > /sk/ > /sl/ > /tv/ > /ps/ > /sp/ > /sv/ > /sm/ > /pfR/ > /pn/ > /gn/ > /sn/ > /fj/ > /sf/
Initial: /St/ > /tR/ > /pR/ > /Sp/ > /kR/ > /Sv/ > /gR/ > /Sl/ > /fR/ > /kl/ > /bR/ > /bl/ > /fl/ > /Sm/ > /gl/ > /tsv/ > /pl/ > /kv/ > /kn/ > /Sn/ > /dR/ > /SR/ > /sk/ > /pfl/ > /ps/ > /gn/ > /sl/ > /sm/ > /sts/ > /sf/ > /sv/ > /ks/ > /tv/ > /vR/ > /sn/ > /mn/ > /st/ > /pn/ > /sp/ > /fj/ > /pfR/ > /mj/
Medial: /St/ > /tR/ > /bR/ > /fR/ > /Sl/ > /gR/ > /kR/ > /bl/ > /dR/ > /Sp/ > /kl/ > /fl/ > /pR/ > /gl/ > /Sv/ > /SR/ > /st/ > /pl/ > /ks/ > /kv/ > /gn/ > /Sn/ > /Sm/ > /kn/ > /tsv/ > /pfl/ > /dl/ > /dn/ > /gm/ > /sp/ > /sn/ > /fn/ > /bn/ > /vj/ > /xR/ > /tn/ > /sl/ > /vR/ > /sk/ > /pj/ > /ps/ > /sts/ > /xn/ > /xl/ > /ml/ > /Rn/ > /Nn/ > /NR/ > /zn/ > /zl/ > /mn/ > /tl/ > /sf/ > /ln/ > /tsR/ > /tsl/ > /sR/ > /ft/ > /zR/ > /pfR/ > /pt/ > /nR/ > /sg/ > /pn/ > /dm/ > /tz/ > /sv/ > /zv/ > /tv/
Final: /St/ > /tR/ > /bl/ > /Sl/ > /bR/ > /fl/ > /kl/ > /dR/ > /gR/ > /Sp/ > /kR/ > /Sv/ > /fR/ > /SR/ > /gl/ > /ks/ > /dl/ > /pl/ > /gn/ > /pR/ > /Sn/ > /Sm/ > /kn/ > /dn/ > /kv/ > /tsv/ > /tl/ > /ml/ > /xl/ > /tsl/ > /gm/ > /pfl/ > /Nl/ > /zl/ > /tn/ > /xR/ > /vR/ > /fn/ > /bn/ > /vj/ > /zn/ > /Nn/ > /pn/ > /RR/ > /mn/ > /xn/ > /zR/ > /NR/ > /lR/ > /dZm/ > /tsR/ > /nl/ > /gv/ > /ps/ > /ft/ > /pfR/ > /tZl/ > /nR/ > /sp/ > /st/ > /sv/ > /sk/ > /sR/ > /sn/ > /sl/ > /sm/ > /sts/

Table 8: Two-consonantal onsets ordered by joint probability (top: English, bottom:German)

5 Discussion

Comparison of the syllabification performance with other systems is difficult: (i) different approaches differ in their training and evaluation corpus; (ii) comparisons across languages are hard to interpret; (iii) comparisons across different approaches require cautious interpretations. Nevertheless, we want to refer to several approaches that examined the syllabification task. Van den Bosch (1997) investigated the syllabification task with five inductive learning algorithms. He reported a generalization error for words of 2.22% on English data. However, the evaluation procedure differs from ours as he evaluates each decision (after each phoneme) made by his algorithms. Marchand et al. (to appear 2006) evaluated different syllabification algorithms on three different pronunciation dictionaries. Their best algorithm (SbA) achieved a word accuracy of 91.08%. The most direct point of comparison are the results presented by Müller (2002). Her approach differs in two ways. First, she only evaluates the German grammar and second she trains on a newspaper corpus. As we are interested in how her grammars perform on our corpus, we re-implemented her grammars and tested both in our 10-fold cross evaluation procedure. We find that the first grammar (Müller, 2001) achieves 85.45% word accuracy, 88.94% syllable accuracy and 94.37% syllable boundary accuracy for English and 84.21%, 90.86%, 95.36% for German respectively. The results show that the syllable boundary accuracy increases from 94,37% to 97.2% for English and from 95.3% to 97.2% for German. The experiments point out that phonotactic knowledge is a valuable source of information for syllabification.

6 Conclusions

Phonotactic restrictions are important for language perception and production. They influence the ability of children to segment words, and they help to recognize words in nonsense sequences. In this paper, we presented grammars which incorporate phonotactic restrictions. The grammars were trained and tested on a German and an English pronunciation dictionary. Our experiments show that English and German profit from phonotactic knowledge to predict syllable boundaries. We find evidence that German codas depend on the nucleus which does not apply for English. The English grammars which model the dependency of part of the onset or coda on the nucleus worsen the syllabification accuracy. However, the combination of both show a better performance than the base phonotactic grammar. This suggests that there are constrains in the selection of the onset and coda consonants.

7 Acknowledgments

I would like to thank Paul Boersma who invited me as a guest researcher at the Institute of Phonetic Sciences of the University of Amsterdam. Special thanks also to Detlef Prescher as well as to the three anonymous reviewers, whose comments were very useful while preparing the final version of this paper.

References

Harald R. Baayen, Richard Piepenbrock, and H. van Rijn. 1993. The CELEX lexical database—Dutch, English, German. (Release 1)[CD-ROM]. Philadelphia, PA: Linguistic Data Consortium, Univ. Pennsylvania.

Anja Belz. 2000. Multi-syllable phonotactic modelling. In *Proceedings of SIGPHON 2000: Finite-State Phonology*, Luxembourg.

Juliette Blevins. 1995. The Syllable in Phonological Theory. In John A. Goldsmith, editor, *Handbook of Phonological Theory*, pages 206–244, Blackwell, Cambridge MA.

Julie Carson-Berndsen, Robert Kelly, and Moritz Neugebauer. 2004. Automatic Acquisition of Feature-Based Phonotactic Resources. In *Proceedings of the Workshop of the ACL Special Interest Group on Computational Phonology (SIGPHON)*, Barcelona, Spain.

Julie Carson-Berndsen. 1998. *Time Map Phonology. Finite State Models and Event Logics in Speech Recognition*, volume 5 of *Text, Speech and Language Technology*. Springer.

Eugene Charniak. 1996. Tree-bank grammars. In *Proceedings of the Thirteenth National Conference on Artificial Intelligence*, AAAI Press/MIT Press, Menlo Park.

Walter Daelemans and Antal van den Bosch. 1992. Generalization performance of backpropagation learning on a syllabification task. In M.F.J. Drossaers and A Nijholt, editors, *Proceedings of TWLT3: Connectionism and Natural Language Processing*, pages 27–37, University of Twente.

Colin J. Ewen and Harry van der Hulst. 2001. *The Phonological Structure of Words. An Introduction*. Cambridge University Press, Cambridge, United Kingdom.

Tracy Hall. 1992. *Syllable structure and syllable related processes in German*. Niemeyer, Tübingen.

Daniel Kahn. 1976. *Syllable-based Generalizations in English Phonology*. Ph.D. thesis, Massachusetts Institute of Technology, MIT.

Brett Kessler and Rebecca Treiman. 1997. Syllable Structure and the Distribuation of Phonemes in English Syllables. *Journal of Memory and Language*, 37:295–311.

George Anton Kiraz and Bernd Möbius. 1998. Multilingual Syllabification Using Weighted Finite-State Transducers. In *Proc. 3rd ESCA Workshop on Speech Synthesis (Jenolan Caves)*, pages 59–64.

Brigitte Krenn. 1997. Tagging syllables. In *Proceedings of the 5th European Conference on Speech Communication and Technology, Eurospeech 97*, pages 991–994.

Yannick Marchand, Connie A. Adsett, and Robert I. Damper. to appear 2006. Automatic syllabification in English: A comparison of different algorithms. *Language and Speech*.

Karin Müller. 2001. Automatic Detection of Syllable Boundaries Combining the Advantages of Treebank and Bracketed Corpora Training. In *Proc. 39th Annual Meeting of the ACL*, Toulouse, France.

Karin Müller. 2002. Probabilistic Context-Free Grammars for Phonology. In *Proceedings of the Workshop on Morphological and Phonological Learning at ACL 2002*.

Janet Pierrehumbert. 1994. Syllable structure and word structure: a study of triconsonantal clusters in English. In Patricia A. Keating, editor, *Phonological Structure and Phonetic Form*, volume III of *Papers in Laboratory Phonology*, pages 168–188. University Press, Cambridge.

Richard Sproat, editor. 1998. *Multilingual Text-to-Speech Synthesis: The Bell Labs Approach*. Kluwer Academic, Dordrecht.

Antal Van den Bosch. 1997. *Learning to Pronounce Written Words: A Study in Inductive Language Learning*. Ph.D. thesis, Univ. Maastricht, Maastricht, The Netherlands.

Jan P.H. Van Santen, Chilin Shih, Bernd Möbius, Evelyne Tzoukermann, and Michael Tanenblatt. 1997. Multilingual duration modeling. In *Proceedings of the European Conference on Speech Communication and Technology (Eurospeech)*, volume 5, pages 2651–2654, Rhodos, Greece.

Michael S. Vitevitch and Paul A. Luce. 1999. Probabilistic Phonotactics and Neighborhood Activation in Spoken Word Recognition. *Journal of Memory and Language*, (40):374–408.

Jean Vroomen, Antal van den Bosch, and Beatrice de Gelder. 1998. A Connectionist Model for Bootstrap Learning of Syllabic Structure. *Language and Cognitive Processes. Special issue on Language Acquisition and Connectionism*, 13(2/3):193–220.

Andrea Weber and Anne Cutler. 2006. First-language phonotactics in second-language listening. *Journal of the Acoustical Society of America*, 119(1):597–607.

Richard Wiese. 1996. *The Phonology of German*. Clarendon Press, Oxford.

Learning Quantity Insensitive Stress Systems via Local Inference

Jeffrey Heinz
Linguistics Department
University of California, Los Angeles
Los Angeles, California 90095
jheinz@humnet.ucla.edu

Abstract

This paper presents an unsupervised batch learner for the quantity-insensitive stress systems described in Gordon (2002). Unlike previous stress learning models, the learner presented here is neither cue based (Dresher and Kaye, 1990), nor reliant on a priori Optimality-theoretic constraints (Tesar, 1998). Instead our learner exploits a property called neighborhood-distinctness, which is shared by all of the target patterns. Some consequences of this approach include a natural explanation for the occurrence of binary and ternary rhythmic patterns, the lack of higher n-ary rhythms, and the fact that, in these systems, stress always falls within a certain window of word edges.

1 Introduction

The central premise of this research is that phonotactic patterns are have properties which reflect properties of the learner. This paper illustrates this approach for quantity-insensitive (QI) stress systems (see below).

I present an unsupervised batch learner that correctly learns every one of these languages. The learner succeeds because there is a universal property of QI stress systems which I refer to as *neighborhood-distinctness* (to be defined below). This property, which is a structural notion of locality, is used by the learning algorithm to successfully infer the target pattern from samples.

A learner is a function from a set of observations to a grammar. An observation is some linguistic sign, in this case a word-sized sequence of stress values. A grammar is some device that must at least respond Yes or No when asked if a linguistic sign is a possible sign for this language (Chomsky and Halle, 1968; Halle, 1978).[1]

The remainder of the introduction outlines the typology of the QI stress systems, motivates representing phonotactics with regular languages, and examines properties of the attested patterns. In §2, I define the class of neighborhood-distinct languages. The learning algorithm is presented in two stages. §3 introduces a basic version of the learner the learner, which successfully acquires just under 90% of the target patterns. In §4, one modification is made to this learner which consequently succeeds on all target patterns. §5 discusses predictions made by these learning algorithms. The appendix summarizes the target patterns and results.

1.1 Quantity-Insensitive Stress Systems

Stress assignment in QI languages is indifferent to the weight of a syllable. For example, Latin is quantity-sensitive (QS) because stress assignment depends on the syllable type: if the penultimate syllable is heavy (i.e. has a long vowel or coda) then it receives stress, but otherwise the antepenult does. The stress systems under consideration here, unlike Latin, do not distinguish syllable types.

[1] In this respect, this work departs from (or is a special case of) gradient phonotactic models (Coleman and Pierrehumbert, 1997; Frisch et al., 2000; Albright, 2006; Hayes and Wilson, 2006)

Proceedings of the Eighth Meeting of the ACL Special Interest Group on Computational Phonology at HLT-NAACL 2006, pages 21–30,
New York City, USA, June 2006.

There are 27 types of QI stress systems found in Gordon's (2002) typology. Gordon adds six plausibly attestable QI systems by considering the behavior of all-light-syllabled words from QS systems.

These 33 patterns are divided into four kinds: single, dual, binary and ternary. Single systems have one stressed syllable per word, and dual systems up to two. Binary and ternary systems stress every second (binary) or third (ternary) syllable.

The choice to study QI stress systems was made for three reasons. First, they are well studied and the typology is well established (Hayes, 1995; Gordon, 2002). Secondly, learning of stress systems has been approached before (Dresher and Kaye, 1990; Gupta and Touretzky, 1991; Goldsmith, 1994; Tesar, 1998) making it possible to compare learners and results. Third, these patterns have been analyzed with adjacency restrictions (e.g. no clash), as disharmony (e.g. a primary stress may not be followed by another), and with recurrence requirements (e.g. build trochaic feet iteratively from the left). Thus the patterns found in the QI stress systems are representative of other phonotactic domains that the learner should eventually be extended to.

The 33 types are shown in Table 1. See Gordon (2002) and Hayes (1995) for details, examples, and original sources. Note that some patterns have a minimal word condition (Prince, 1980; McCarthy and Prince, 1990; Hayes, 1995), banning either monosyllables or light monosyllables. For example, Cayuvava bans all monosyllables, whereas Hopi bans only light monosyllables. Because this paper addresses QI stress patterns I abstract away from the internal structure of the syllable. For convenience, when stress patterns are explicated in this paper I assume (stressed) monosyllables are permitted. The learning study, however, includes each stress pattern both with and without stressed monosyllables. Predictions our learner makes with respect to the minimal word condition are given in §5.2.

[2]We use the (first) language name to exemplify the stress pattern. The number in parentheses is an index to the language Gordon's 2003 appendix. All stress representations follow Gordon's notation, who uses the metrical grid (Liberman and Prince, 1977; Prince, 1983). Thus, primary stress is indicated by 2, secondary stress by 1, and no stress by 0.

1.2 Phonotactics as Regular Languages

I represent phonotactic descriptions as regular sets, accepted by finite-state machines. A finite state machine is a 5-tuple $(\Sigma, Q, q_0, F, \delta)$ where Σ is a finite alphabet, Q is a set of states, $q_0 \in Q$ is the start state, $F \subseteq Q$ is a set of final states, and δ is a set of transitions. Each transition has an origin and a terminus and is labeled with a symbol of the alphabet; i.e. a transition is a 3-tuple (o, a, t) where $o, t \in Q$ and $a \in \Sigma$.

Empirically, it has been observed that most phonological phenomena are regular (Johnson, 1972; Kaplan and Kay, 1981; Kaplan and Kay, 1994; Ellison, 1994; Eisner, 1997; Karttunen, 1998). This is especially true of phonotactics: reduplication and metathesis, which have higher complexity, are not phonotactic patterns as they involve alternations.[3]

Formally, regular languages are widely studied in computer science, and their basic properties are well understood (Hopcroft et al., 2001). Also, a learning literature exists. E.g. the class of regular languages is not exactly identifiable in the limit (Gold, 1967), but certain subsets of it are (Angluin, 1980; Angluin, 1982). Thus it is becomes possible to ask: What subset of the regular languages delimits the class of possible human phonotactics and can properties of this class be exploited by a learner?

This perspective also connects to finite state models of Optimality Theory (OT) (Prince and Smolensky, 1993). Riggle (2004) shows that if OT constraints are made finite-state, it is possible to build a transducer that takes any input to a grammatical output. Removing from this transducer the input labels and hidden structural symbols (such as foot boundaries) in the output labels yields a phonotactic acceptor for the language, a target for our learner.

Consider Pintupi, #26 in Table 1, which exemplifies a binary stress pattern. Its phonotactic grammar is given in Figure 1. The hexagon indicates the start state, and final states are marked by the double perimeter.

This machine accepts the Pintupi words, but not other words of the same length. Also, the Pintupi grammar accepts an infinite number of words– just like the grammars in Hayes (1995) and Gordon

[3]See Albro (1998; 2005) for restricted extensions to regular languages.

Table 1: The Quantity-Insensitive Stress Systems.[2]

		Single Systems							
1.	(1) Chitimacha	20000000	2000000	200000	20000	2000	200	20	2
2.	(2) Lakota	02000000	0200000	020000	02000	0200	020	02	2
3.	(3) Hopi (qs)	02000000	0200000	020000	02000	0200	020	20	2
4.	(4) Macedonian	00000200	0000200	000200	00200	0200	200	20	2
5.	(5) Nahuatl / Mohawk†	00000020	0000020	000020	00020	0020	020	20	2
6.	(6) Atayal / Diegueño‡	00000002	0000002	000002	00002	0002	002	02	2
		Dual Systems							
7.	(7f) Quebec French	10000002	1000002	100002	10002	1002	102	12	2
8.	(9f) Udihe	10000002	1000002	100002	10002	1002	102	02	2
9.	(10i) Lower Sorbian	20000010	2000010	200010	20010	2010	200	20	2
10.	(11f) Sanuma	10000020	1000020	100020	10020	1020	020	20	2
11.	(15f) Georgian	10000200	1000200	100200	10200	0200	200	20	2
12.	(16i) Walmatjari	20000100	2000100	200100	20100	2010	200	20	2
	(optional variants)	20000010	2000010	200010	20010				
		Binary Systems							
13.	(24i) Araucanian	02010101	0201010	020101	02010	0201	020	02	2
14.	(24f) Creek‡ (qs)	01010102	0101020	010102	01020	0102	020	02	2
15.	(25f) Urubu Kaapor	01010102	1010102	010102	10102	0102	102	02	2
16.	(26i) Malakmalak	20101010	0201010	201010	02010	2010	020	20	2
17.	(26f) Cavineña†	10101020	0101020	101020	01020	1020	020	20	2
18.	(27i) Maranungku	20101010	2010101	201010	20101	2010	201	20	2
19.	(27f) Palestinean Arabic‡ (qs)	10101020	1010102	101020	10102	1020	102	20	2
		Binary Systems with Clash							
20.	(28i) Central Alaskan Yupik‡	01010102	0101012	010102	01012	0102	012	02	2
21.	(29i) Southern Paiute‡	02010110	0201010	020110	02010	0210	020	20	2
22.	(30i) Gosiute Shoshone	20101011	2010101	201011	20101	2011	201	21	2
23.	(32f) Biangai	10101020	1101020	101020	11020	1020	120	20	2
24.	(33f) Tauya	11010102	1010102	110102	10102	1102	102	12	2
		Binary Systems with Lapse							
25.	(34f) Piro	10101020	1010020	101020	10020	1020	020	20	2
26.	(36i) Pintupi / Diyari†	20101010	2010100	201010	20100	2010	200	20	2
27.	(40f) Indonesian	10101020	1001020	101020	10020	1020	020	20	2
28.	(42i) Garawa	20101010	2001010	201010	20010	2010	200	20	2
		Ternary Systems							
29.	(48i) Ioway-Oto	02001001	0200100	020010	02001	0200	020	02	2
30.	(49f) Cayuvava†	00100200	0100200	100200	00200	0200	200	20	2
31.	(67i) Estonian (qs)	20010010	2001010	201010	20010	2010	200	20	2
	(optional variants)	20101010	2010100	200100	20100				
		20100100	2010010						
		20010100							
32.	(71f) Pacific Yupik (qs)	01001002	0100102	010020	01002	0102	020	02	2
33.	(72i) Winnebago‡ (qs)	00200101	0020010	002001	00201	0020	002	02	2

† Bans monosyllables.

‡ Bans light monosyllables.

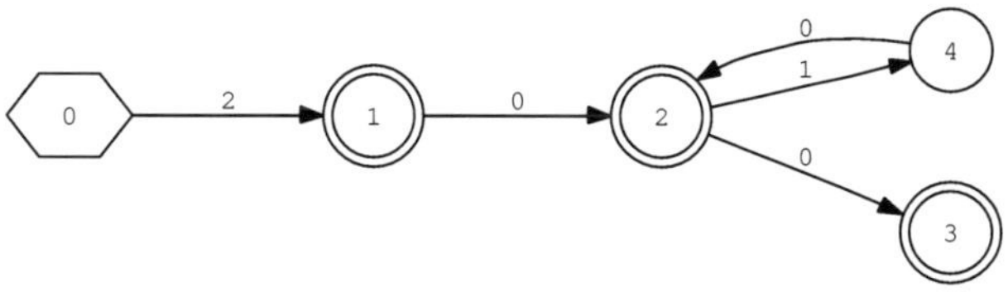

Figure 1: Stress in Pintupi as a finite state machine

(2002), who take the observed forms as instances of a pattern that extends to longer words. The learner's task is to take the Pintupi words in Table 1 and return the pattern represented by Figure 1.

1.3 Properties of QI Stress Patterns

The deterministic acceptor with the fewest states for a language is called the language's canonical acceptor. Therefore, let us ask what properties the canonical acceptors for the 33 stress types have in common that might be exploited by a learner.

One property shared by all grammars except Estonian is that they have exactly one loop (Estonian has two). Though this restriction is nontrivial, it is insufficient for learning to be guaranteed.[4] A second shared property is *slenderness*. A machine is slender iff it accepts only one word of length n. The only exceptions to this are Walmatjari and Estonian, which have free variation in longer words (see Table 1).

I focus in this paper on another property which are shared by all machines without exception. In 29 of the canonical acceptors, each state can be uniquely identified by its incoming symbol set, its outgoing symbol set, and whether it is final or non-final. These items make up the *neighborhood* of a state, which will be formally defined in the next section. The other four stress systems have non-canonical acceptors wherein each state can also be uniquely identified by its neighborhood. This property I call *neighborhood-distinctness*. Thus, neighborhood-distinctness is a universal property of QI stress systems, and it is this property that the learner will exploit.

[4]The proof is similar to the one used to show the cofinite languages are not learnable (Osherson et al., 1986).

2 Neighborhood-Distinctness

2.1 Neighborhood-Distinct Acceptors

The neighborhood of a state in an acceptor $(\Sigma, Q, q_0, F, \delta)$ is defined in (1).

(1) The **neighborhood** of a state q is triple (f, I, O) where $f = 1$ iff $q \in F$ and $f = 0$ otherwise, $I = \{a \mid \exists o \in Q,\ (o, a, q) \in \delta\}$, and $O = \{a \mid \exists t \in Q,\ (q, a, t) \in \delta\}$

Thus the neighborhood of state can be determined by looking solely at whether or not it is final, the set of symbols labeling the transitions which reach that state, and the set of symbols labeling the transitions which depart that state. For example in Figure 2, states p and q have the same neighborhood because they are both nonfinal, can both be reached by some element of $\{a, b\}$, and because each state can only be exited by observing a member of $\{c, d\}$.[5]

Figure 2: Two states with the same neighborhood.

Neighborhood-distinct acceptors are defined in (2).

(2) An acceptor is said to be **neighborhood-distinct** iff no two states have the same neighborhood.

This class of acceptors is finite: there are $2^{2|\Sigma|+1}$ neighborhoods, i.e. types of states. Since each state in a neighborhood-distinct machine has a unique neighborhood, this becomes an upper bound on machine size.[6]

[5]The notion of neighborhood can be generalized to neighborhoods of size k, where sets I and O are defined as the incoming and outgoing paths of length k. However, this paper is only concerned with neighborhoods of size 1.

[6]For some acceptor, the notion of neighborhood lends itself to an equivalence relation R_N over Q: pR_Nq iff p and q have the same neighborhood. Therefore, R_N partitions Q into blocks, and neighborhood-distinct machines are those where this partition equals the trivial partition.

2.2 Neighborhood-Distinct Languages

The class of neighborhood-distinct languages is defined in (3).

(3) **The neighborhood-distinct languages** are those for which there is an acceptor which is neighborhood-distinct.

The neighborhood-distinct languages are a (finite) proper subset of the regular languages over an alphabet Σ: all regular languages whose smallest acceptors have more than $2^{2|\Sigma|+1}$ states cannot be neighborhood-distinct (since at least two states would have the same neighborhood).

The canonically neighborhood-distinct languages are defined in (4).

(4) **The canonically neighborhood-distinct languages** are those for which the canonical acceptor is neighborhood-distinct.

The canonically neighborhood-distinct languages form a proper subset of the neighborhood-distinct languages. For example, the canonical acceptor shown in Figure 3 of Lower Sorbian (#9 in Table 1) is not neighborhood-distinct (states 2 and 3 have the same neighborhood). However, there is a non-canonical (because non-deterministic) neighborhood-distinct acceptor for this language, as shown in Figure 4.

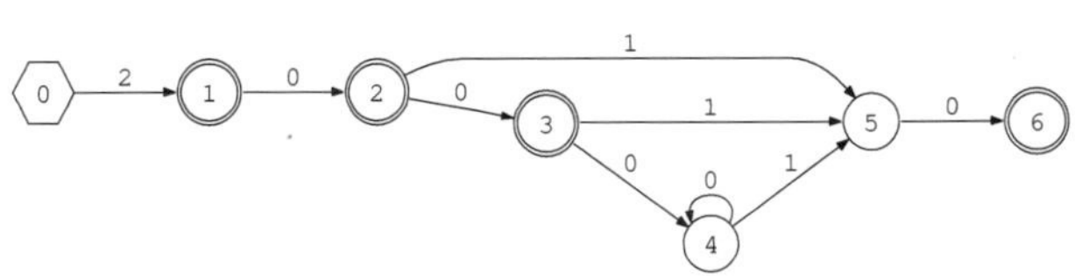

Figure 3: The canonical acceptor for Lower Sorbian.

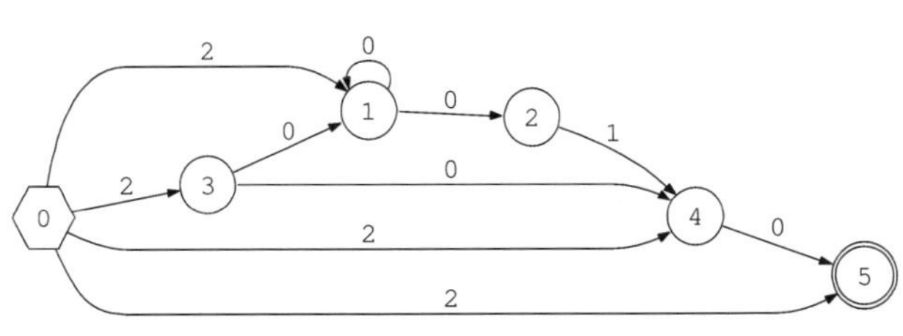

Figure 4: A neighborhood-distinct acceptor for Lower Sorbian.

Neighborhood-distinctness is a universal property of the patterns under consideration. Additionally, it is a property which a learner can use to induce a grammar from surface forms.

3 The Neighborhood Learner

In this section, I present the basic unsupervised batch learner, called the Neighborhood Learner, which learns 29 of the 33 patterns. In the next section, I introduce one modification to this learner which results in perfect accuracy.

The basic version of the learner operates in two stages: prefix tree construction and state-merging, cf. Angluin (1982). These two stages find smaller descriptions of the observed data; in particular state-merging may lead to generalization (see below).

A prefix tree is constructed as follows. Set the initial machine $M = (\Sigma, \{q_0\}, q_0, \emptyset, \emptyset)$ and the current state $c = q_0$. With each word, each symbol a is considered in order. If $\forall t \in Q$, $(c, a, t) \in \delta$ then set $c = t$. Otherwise, add a new state n to Q and a new arc (c, a, n) to δ. A new arc is therefore created on every symbol in the first word. The last state for a word is added to F. The process is repeated for each word. The prefix tree for Pintupi words from Table 1 is shown in Figure 5.

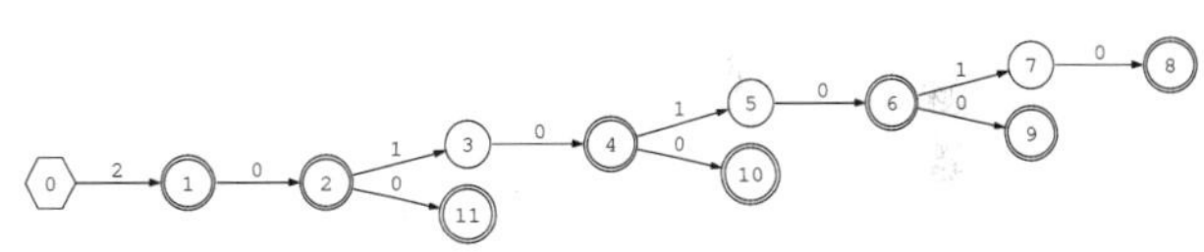

Figure 5: The prefix tree of Pintupi words.

The second stage of the learner is state-merging, a process which reduces the number of states in the machine. A key concept in state merging is that when two states are merged into a single state, their transitions are preserved. Specifically, if states p and q merge, then a merged state pq is added to the machine, and p and q are removed. For every arc that left p (or q) to a state r, there is now an arc from pq going to r. Likewise, for every arc from a state r to p (or q), there is now an arc from r to pq.

The post-merged machine accepts every word that the pre-merged machine accepts, and possibly more. For example, if there is a path between two states which become merged, a loop is formed.

What remains to be explained is the criteria the learner uses to determine whether two states in the prefix tree merge. The Neighborhood Learner merges two states iff they have the same neighborhood, guaranteeing that the resulting grammar is neighborhood-distinct.

The intuition is that the prefix tree provides a structured representation of the input and has recorded information about different environments, which are represented in the tree as states. Learning is a process which identifies actually different environments as 'the same'— here states are 'the same' iff their local features, i.e their neighborhoods, are the same. For example, suppose states p and q in the prefix tree are both final or both nonfinal, and they share the same incoming symbol set and outgoing symbol set. In the learner's eyes they are then 'the same', and will be merged.

The merging criteria partitions the states of the Pintupi prefix tree into five groups. States 3,5 and 7 are merged; states 2,4,6 are merged, and states 8,9,10,12 are merged. Merging of states halts when no two nodes have the same neighborhood– thus, the resulting machine is neighborhood-distinct. The result for Pintupi is shown in Figure 6.

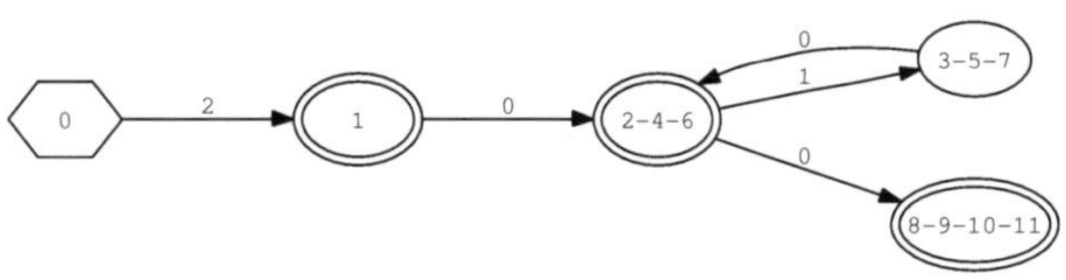

Figure 6: The grammar learned for Pintupi.

The machine in Figure 6 is equivalent to the one in Figure 1– they accept exactly the same language.[7] I.e. neighborhood merging of the prefix tree in Figure 5 generalizes from the data exactly as desired.

3.1 Results of Neighborhood Learning

The Neighborhood Learner successfully learns 29 of the 33 language types (see appendix). These are exactly the 29 canonically neighborhood-distinct languages. This suggests the following claim, which has not been proven.[8]

(5) **Conjecture:** The Neighborhood Learner identifies the class of canonically neighborhood-distinct languages.

In §4, I discuss why the learner fails where it does, and introduce a modification which results in perfect accuracy.

4 Reversing the Prefix Tree

This section examines the four cases where neighborhood learning failed and modifies the learning algorithm, resulting in perfect accuracy. The goal is to restrict generalization because in every case where learning failed, the learner overgeneralized by merging more states than it should have. Thus, the resulting grammars recognize multiple words with n syllables.

The dual stress pattern of Lower Sorbian places stress initially and, in words of four or more syllables, on the penult (see #9 Table 1). The prefix tree built from these words is shown in Figure 7.

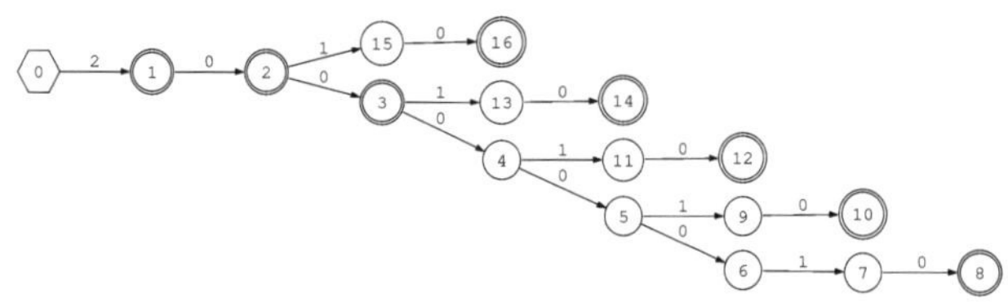

Figure 7: The prefix tree for Lower Sorbian.

Here the Neighborhood Learner fails because it merges states 2 and 3. The resulting grammar incorrectly accepts words of the form 20*.

The proposed solution follows from the observation that if the prefix tree were constructed in reverse (reading each word from right to left) then the corresponding states in this structure would not have the same neighborhoods, and thus not be merged. A reverse prefix tree is constructed like a forward prefix tree, the only difference being that the order of symbols in each word is reversed. When neighborhood learning is applied to this structure and the resulting machine reversed again, the correct grammar is obtained, shown in Figure 4.

How is the learner to know whether to construct the prefix tree normally or in reverse? It simply does both and intersects the results. Intersection of two

[7] This can be verified by checking to see if the minimized versions of the two machines are isomorphic.

[8] The proof is made difficult by the fact that the acceptor returned by the Neighborhood Learner is not necessarily the canonical acceptor.

languages is an operation which returns a language consisting of the words common to both. Similarly, machine intersection returns an acceptor which recognizes just those words that both machines recognize. This strategy is thus conservative: the learner keeps only the most robust generalizations, which are the ones it 'finds' in both the forward and reverse prefix trees.

This new learner is called the Forward Backward Neighborhood (FBN) Learner and it succeeds with all the patterns (see appendix).

Interestingly, the additional languages the FBN Learner can acquire are ones that, under foot-based analyses like those in Hayes (1995), require feet to be built from the right word edge. For example, Lower Sorbian has a binary trochee aligned to the right word edge; Indonesian iteratively builds binary trochaic feet from the right word edge; Cayuvava iteratively builds anapests from the right word edge. Thus structuring the input in reverse appears akin to a footing procedure which proceeds from the right word boundary.

5 Predictions of Neighborhood Learning

In this section, let us examine some of the predictions that are made by neighborhood learning. In particular, let us consider the kinds of languages that the Neighborhood Learner can and cannot learn and compare them with the attested typology.

5.1 Binary and Ternary Stress Patterns

Neighborhood learning suggests an explanation of the fact that the stress rhythms found in natural language are binary or ternary and not higher n-ary, and of the fact that stress falls within a three-syllable window of the word edge: perhaps only systems with these properties are learnable. This is because the neighborhood learner cannot distinguish between sequences of the same symbol with length greater than two.

As an example, consider the quaternary (and higher n-ary) stress pattern $2(0001)^*(0|00|000)$.[9] If the learner is exposed to samples from this pattern, it incorrectly generalizes to $2(000^*1)^*(0|00|000)$.

[9]I follow Hopcroft et al (2001) in our notation of regular expressions with one substitution– we use | instead of + to indicate disjunction.

Similarly, neighborhood learning cannot distinguish a form like 02000 from 020000, so a system that places stress on the pre-antepenult (e.g. 02000, 002000, 0002000) is not learnable. With samples from the pre-antepenultimate language $(0^*2000|200|20|2)$, the learner incorrectly generalizes to 0^*20^*.

5.2 Minimal Word Conditions

A subtle prediction made by neighborhood-learning is that a QI stress language with a pattern like the one exemplified by Hopi (shown in Figure 8) cannot have a minimal word condition banning monosyllables. This is because if there were no monosyllables in this language, then state 4 in Figure 8 would have the same neighborhood as state 2 (as in Figure 9).

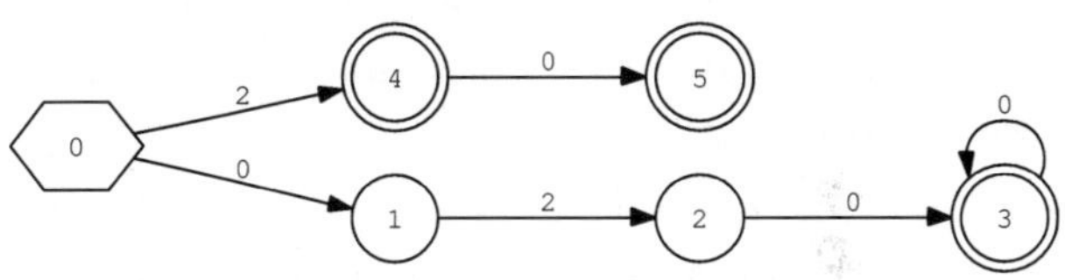

Figure 8: The stress pattern exemplified by Hopi, allowing monosyllables.

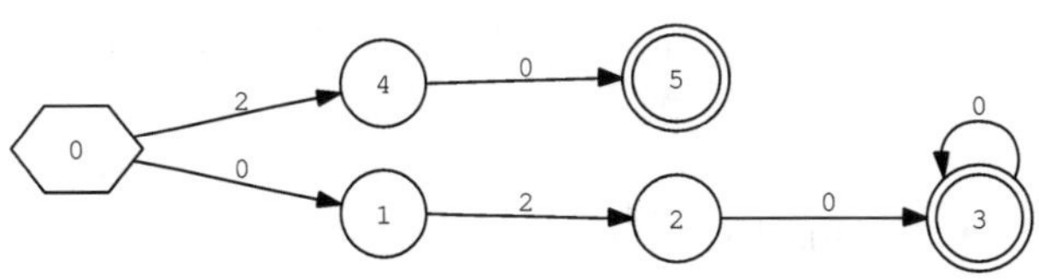

Figure 9: The stress pattern exemplified by Hopi, not allowing monosyllables.

Since such a grammar recognizes a non-neighborhood-distinct language it cannot be learned by the Neighborhood Learner.

As it happens, Hopi is a QS language which prohibits light, but permits heavy, monosyllables. Since I have abstracted away from the internal structure of the syllable in this paper, this prediction is not disconfirmed by the known typology: there are in fact no QI Hopi-like stress patterns in Gordon's (2002) typology which ban all monosyllables; i.e there are no QI patterns like the one in Figure 9.

Some QI languages do have a minimal word condition banning all monosyllables. To our knowledge these are Cavineña and Cayuvava (see Table 1), Mohawk (which places stress on the penult like Nahuatl), and Diyari, Mohwak, Pitta Pitta and Wangkumara (all which assign stress like Pintupi) (Hayes, 1995). The Forward Backward Neighborhood Learner learns all of these patterns successfully irrespective of whether the patterns (and corresponding input samples) permit monosyllables, predicting that such patterns do not correlate with a prohibition on monosyllables (see appendix).

Other QI languages prohibit light monosyllables. Diegueño, for example, places stress finally like Atayal (see Table 1), but only allows heavy monosyllables. This is an issue to attend to in future research when trying to extend the learning algorithm to QS patterns, when the syllable type (light/heavy) is included in the representational scheme.

5.3 Restrictiveness and Other Approaches

There are languages that can be learned by neighborhood learning that phonologists do not consider to be natural. For example, the Neighborhood Learner learns a pattern in which words with an odd number of syllables bear initial stress but words with an even number of syllables bear stress on all odd syllables. However, the grammar for this language differs from all of the attested systems in that it has two loops but is slender (cf. Estonian which has two loops but is not slender). Thus this case suggests a further formal restriction to the class of possible stress systems.

More serious challenges of unattestable, but Neighborhood Learner-able, patterns exist; e.g. 21*. In other words, it does not follow from neighborhood-distinctness that languages with stress must have stressless syllables. Nor does the notion that every word must bear some stress somewhere (i.e. Culminativity– see Hayes (1995)).

However, despite the existence of learnable pathological languages, this approach is not unrestricted. The class of languages to be learned is finite—as in the Optimality-theoretic and Principles and Parameters frameworks—and is a proper subset of the regular languages. Future research will seek additional properties to better approximate the class of QI stress systems that can be exploited by inductive learning.

This approach offers more insight into QI stress systems than earlier learning models. Optimality-theoretic learning models (e.g. (Tesar, 1998)) and models set in the Principles and Parameters framework (e.g. (Dresher and Kaye, 1990)) make no use of any property of the class of patterns to be learned beyond its finiteness. Also, our learner is much simpler than these other models, which require a large set of a priori switches and cues or constraints.

6 Conclusions

This paper presented a batch learner which correctly infers the attested QI stress patterns from surface forms. The key to the success of this learner is that it takes advantage of a universal property of QI stress systems, neighborhood-distinctness. This property provides a natural explanation for why stress falls within a particular window of the word edge and why rhythms are binary and ternary. It is striking that all of the attested patterns are learned by this simple approach, suggesting that it will be fruitful and revealing when applied to other phonotactic learning problems.

Acknowledgements

I especially thank Bruce Hayes, Ed Stabler, Colin Wilson, Kie Zuraw and the anonymous reviewers for insightful comments and suggestions. I also thank Sarah Churng, Greg Kobele, Katya Pertsova, and Sarah VanWagenen for helpful discussion.

References

Adam Albright. 2006. Gradient phonotactic effects: lexical? grammatical? both? neither? Talk handout from the 80th Annual LSA Meeting, Albuquerque, NM.

Dan Albro. 1998. Evaluation, implementation, and extension of primitive optimality theory. Master's thesis, University of California, Los Angeles.

Dan Albro. 2005. *A Large-Scale, LPM-OT Analysis of Malagasy*. Ph.D. thesis, University of California, Los Angeles.

Dana Angluin. 1980. Finding patterns common to a set of strings. *Journal of Computer and System Sciences*, 21:46–62.

Dana Angluin. 1982. Inference of reversible languages. *Journal for the Association of Computing Machinery*, 29(3):741–765.

Noam Chomsky and Morris Halle. 1968. *The Sound Pattern of English*. Harper & Row.

John Coleman and Janet Pierrehumbert. 1997. Stochastic phonological grammars and acceptability. In *Compuational Phonolgy*, pages 49–56. Somerset, NJ: Association for Computational Linguistics. Third Meeting of the ACL Special Interest Group in Computational Phonology.

Elan Dresher and Jonathan Kaye. 1990. A computational learning model for metrical phonology. *Cognition*, 34:137–195.

Jason Eisner. 1997. What constraints should ot allow? Talk handout, Linguistic Society of America, Chicago, January. Available on the Rutgers Optimality Archive, ROA#204-0797, http://roa.rutgers.edu/.

T.M. Ellison. 1994. The iterative learning of phonological constraints. *Computational Linguistics*, 20(3).

S. Frisch, N.R. Large, and D.B. Pisoni. 2000. Perception of wordlikeness: Effects of segment probability and length on the processing of nonwords. *Journal of Memory and Language*, 42:481–496.

E.M. Gold. 1967. Language identification in the limit. *Information and Control*, 10:447–474.

John Goldsmith. 1994. A dynamic computational theory of accent systems. In Jennifer Cole and Charles Kisseberth, editors, *Perspectives in Phonology*, pages 1–28. Stanford: Center for the Study of Language and Information.

Matthew Gordon. 2002. A factorial typology of quantity-insensitive stress. *Natural Language and Linguistic Theory*, 20(3):491–552. Appendices available at http://www.linguistics.ucsb.edu/faculty/gordon/pubs.html.

Prahlad Gupta and David Touretzky. 1991. What a perceptron reveals about metrical phonology. In *Proceedings of the Thirteenth Annual Conference of the Cognitive Science Society*, pages 334–339.

Morris Halle. 1978. Knowledge unlearned and untaught: What speakers know about the sounds of their language. In *Linguistic Theory and Psychological Reality*. The MIT Prss.

Bruce Hayes and Colin Wilson. 2006. The ucla phonotactic learner. Talk handout from UCLA Phonology Seminar.

Bruce Hayes. 1995. *Metrical Stress Theory*. Chicago University Press.

John Hopcroft, Rajeev Motwani, and Jeffrey Ullman. 2001. *Introduction to Automata Theory, Languages, and Computation*. Addison-Wesley.

C. Douglas Johnson. 1972. *Formal Aspects of Phonological Description*. The Hague: Mouton.

Ronald Kaplan and Martin Kay. 1981. Phonological rules and finite state transducers. Paper presented at ACL/LSA Conference, New York.

Ronald Kaplan and Martin Kay. 1994. Regular models of phonological rule systems. *Computational Linguistics*, 20(3):331–378.

Lauri Karttunen. 1998. The proper treatment of optimality theory in computational phonology. *Finite-state methods in natural language processing*, pages 1–12.

Mark Liberman and Alan Prince. 1977. On stress and linguistic rhythm. *Linguistic Inquiry*, 8:249–336.

John McCarthy and Alan Prince. 1990. Foot and word in prosodic morphology. *Natural Language and Linguistic Theory*, 8:209–283.

Daniel Osherson, Scott Weinstein, and Michael Stob. 1986. *Systems that Learn*. MIT Press, Cambridge, Massachusetts.

Alan Prince and Paul Smolensky. 1993. Optimality theory: Constraint interaction in generative grammar. Technical Report 2, Rutgers University Center for Cognitive Science.

Alan Prince. 1980. A metrical theory for estonian quantity. *Linguistic Inquiry*, 11:511–562.

Alan Prince. 1983. Relating to the grid. *Linguistic Inquiry*, 14(1).

Jason Riggle. 2004. *Generation, Recognition, and Learning in Finite State Optimality Theory*. Ph.D. thesis, University of California, Los Angeles.

Bruce Tesar. 1998. An interative strategy for language learning. *Lingua*, 104:131–145.

Appendix. Target Grammars and Results

See Table 2. Circled numbers mean the learner identified the pattern. The $\times$ mark means the learner failed to identify the pattern. The number inside the circle indicates which forms were necessary for convergence. Specifically, in the "With Monosyllables" column, ⓝ means the learner succeeded learning the "With Monosyllables" pattern with words with one to n syllables. Likewise, in the "Without Monosyllables" column, ⓝ means the learner succeeded learning the "Without Monosyllables" pattern with words with two to n syllables. For example, in the "With Monosyllables" column, ⑤ means that the learner succeeded only with words with one to five syllables. The learners still succeed when given longer words. The number n may be thought of as the smallest word needed for generalization.

Table 2: Learning Results

	Language	With Monosyllables RegExp	NHL	FBNL	Without Monosyllables RegExp	NHL	FBNL
		Single					
1.	Chitimacha	20^*	④	④	20^+	④	④
2.	Lakota	$(2 \mid 020^*)$	⑤	⑤	020^*	⑤	⑤
3.	Hopi (qs)	$(2 \mid 20 \mid 020^+)$	⑤	⑤	$(020^* \mid 2)0$	×	×
4.	Macedonian	$(2 \mid 20 \mid 0^*200)$	⑥	⑥	$(2 \mid 0^*20)0$	×	⑥
5.	Nahuatl	$(2 \mid 0^*20)$	⑤	⑤	0^*20	⑤	⑤
6.	Atayal	0^*2	④	④	0^+2	④	④
		Dual					
7.	Quebec French	$(2 \mid 10^*2)$	⑤	⑤	10^*2	⑤	⑤
8.	Udihe	$(2 \mid (10^*)^?02)$	⑤	⑥	$(10^*)^?02$	⑤	⑥
9.	Lower Sorbian	$(2 \mid 2(0 \mid 0^+1)0)$	×	⑥	$2(0 \mid 0^+1)0$	×	⑥
10.	Sanuma	$(2 \mid 20 \mid 020 \mid 10^+20)$	⑥	⑦	$(2 \mid 02 \mid 10^+2)0$	⑥	⑦
11.	Georgian	$(2 \mid 20 \mid 0^?200 \mid 10^+200)$	⑦	⑧	$(2 \mid 0^?20 \mid 10^+20)0$	×	⑧
12.	Walmatjari	$(2 \mid 20(0^*10)^?0^?)$	×	⑥	$20(0^*10)^?0^?$	×	⑥
		Binary					
13.	Araucanian	$(2 \mid 02(01)^*0^?)$	⑥	⑥	$02(01)^*0^?$	⑥	⑥
14.	Creek (qs)	$(2 \mid (01)^*020^?)$	⑥	⑥	$(01)^*020^?$	⑥	⑥
15.	Urubu Kappor	$0^?(10)^*2$	⑤	⑤	$(0 \mid 10)(10)^*2$	⑤	⑤
16.	Malakmalak	$(2 \mid 0^?2(01)^*0)$	⑥	⑥	$0^?2(01)^*0$	⑥	⑥
17.	Cavineña	$(2 \mid 0^?(10)^*20)$	⑥	⑥	$0^?(10)^*20$	⑥	⑥
18.	Maranungku	$2(01)^*0^?$	⑤	⑤	$20(10)^*1^?$	⑤	⑤
19.	Palestinean Arabic (qs)	$(10)^*20^?$	⑤	⑤	$(20 \mid (10)^+20^?)$	⑤	⑤
		Binary w/clash					
20.	Central Alaskan Yupik	$(0(10)^*1^?)^?2$	⑤	⑤	$0(10)^*1^?2$	⑤	⑤
21.	Southern Paiute	$(2 \mid (2 \mid 02(01) * 1^?)0)$	⑦	⑧	$(2 \mid 02(01) * 1^?)0$	⑦	⑧
22.	Gosiute Shoshone	$2((01)^*0^?1)^?$	⑤	⑥	$2(01)^*0^?1$	⑤	⑥
23.	Biangai	$(2 \mid 1^?(10)^*20)$	⑦	⑦	$1^?(10)^*20$	⑦	⑦
24.	Tauya	$(2 \mid 1^?(10)^*2)$	⑥	⑥	$1^?(10)^*2$	⑥	⑥
		Binary w/lapse					
25.	Piro	$(2 \mid (10)^*0^?20)$	⑥	⑦	$(10)^*0^?20$	⑥	⑦
26.	Pintupi	$2(0(10)^*0^?)^?$	⑥	⑥	$20(10)^*0^?$	⑥	⑥
27.	Indonesian	$(2 \mid (10)^?0^?(10)^*20)$	×	⑧	$(10)^?0^?(10)^*20$	×	⑧
28.	Garawa	$2(00^?(10)^*)^?$	⑥	⑥	$200^?(10)^*$	⑥	⑥
		Ternary					
29.	Ioway Oto	$(2 \mid 02(001)^*0^?0^?)$	⑦	⑧	$02(001)^*0^?0^?$	⑦	⑧
30.	Cayuvava	$(0^?0^?(100)^*200 \mid 20 \mid 2)$	×	⑨	$(0^?0^?(100)^*20 \mid 2)0$	×	⑨
31.	Estonian (qs)	$20^?0^?(100 \mid 10)^*$	⑥	⑥	$200^?(100 \mid 10)^*$	⑥	⑥
32.	Pacific Yupik (qs)	$(2 \mid 0(100)^*(20^? \mid 102))$	⑦	⑦	$0(100)^*(20^? \mid 102)$	⑦	⑦
33.	Winnebago (qs)	$(2 \mid 02 \mid 002(001)^*0^?1^?)$	⑨	⑨	$(02 \mid 002(001)^*0^?1^?)$	⑨	⑨

NHL : Neighborhood Learner   FBNL : Forward Backward Neighborhood Learner

Invited Talk: Universal Constraint Rankings Result from Learning and Evolution

Paul Boersma
Institute of Phonetic Sciences
University of Amsterdam
Herengracht 338
1016CG Amsterdam, The Netherlands
paul.boersma@uva.nl

Abstract

Optimality Theory has met with a bad press in the more emergentist (e.g. computational) literature for its reliance on innate constraints and even on innate constraint rankings (positional faithfulness, licensing by cue). In this talk I will show with computer simulations that even if the learner's initial grammar starts with a large number of constraints that have no inherent bias towards unmarked or otherwise good sound systems, the learner will gradually turn the constraint ranking into something resembling a universally unmarked sound system as an automatic result of input frequencies and imperfections of the transmission channel. It turns out that the parents' sound system is "semi-learnable": if the parents' sound system happens to be universally marked, the offspring will learn to mimic the quirks of this system to some extent, but they will tend to turn the language into a universally unmarked sound system within three generations or so. The conclusion will be that a bidirectional Optimality-Theoretic model of the grammar with two phonological and two phonetic representations is compatible with the view that there is no innate phonological substance in language acquisition.

Proceedings of the Eighth Meeting of the ACL Special Interest Group on Computational Phonology at HLT-NAACL 2006, page 31,
New York City, USA, June 2006.

Exploring variant definitions of pointer length in MDL

Aris Xanthos
Department of Linguistics
University of Chicago
Chicago IL 60637
axanthos@uchicago.edu

Yu Hu
Department of
Computer Science
University of Chicago
Chicago IL 60637
yuhu@uchicago.edu

John Goldsmith
Departments of Linguistics and
Computer Science
University of Chicago
Chicago IL 60637
goldsmith@uchicago.edu

Abstract

Within the information-theoretical framework described by (Rissanen, 1989; de Marcken, 1996; Goldsmith, 2001), pointers are used to avoid repetition of phonological material. Work with which we are familiar has assumed that there is only one way in which items could be pointed to. The purpose of this paper is to describe and compare several different methods, each of which satisfies MDL's basic requirements, but which have different consequences for the treatment of linguistic phenomena. In particular, we assess the conditions under which these different ways of pointing yield more compact descriptions of the data, both from a theoretical and an empirical perspective.

1 Introduction

The fundamental hypothesis underlying the *Minimum Description Length* (*MDL*) framework (Rissanen, 1989; de Marcken, 1996; Goldsmith, 2001) is that the selection of a model for explaining a set of data should aim at satisfying two constraints: on the one hand, it is desirable to select a model that can be described in a highly compact fashion; on the other hand, the selected model should make it possible to model the data well, which is interpreted as being able to describe the data in a maximally compact fashion. In order to turn this principle into an operational procedure, it is necessary to make explicit the notion of *compactness*. This is not a trivial problem, as the compactness (or conversely, the *length*) of a description depends not only on the complexity of the object being described (in this case, either a model or a set of data given a model), but also on the "language" that is used for the description.

Consider, for instance, the model of morphology described in Goldsmith (2001). In this work, the data consist in a (symbolically transcribed) corpus segmented into words, and the "language" used to describe the data contains essentially three objects: a list of *stems*, a list of *suffixes*, and a list of *signatures*, i.e. structures specifying which stems associate with which suffixes to form the words found in the corpus. The length of a particular model (or *morphology*) is defined as the sum of the lengths of the three lists that compose it; the length of each list is in turn defined as the sum of the lengths of elements in it, plus a small cost for the list structure itself[1]. The length of an individual morpheme (stem or suffix) is taken to be proportional to the number of symbols in it.

Calculating the length of a signature involves the notion of *pointer*, with which this paper is primarily concerned. The function of a signature is to relate a number of stems with a number of suffixes. Since each of these morphemes is spelled once in the corresponding list, there is no need to spell it again in a signature that contains it. Rather, each signature comprises a list of pointers to stems and a list of pointers to suffixes. A pointer is a symbol that *stands for* a particular morpheme, and the recourse to pointers relies on the assumption that

[1]More on this in section 2.1 below

Proceedings of the Eighth Meeting of the ACL Special Interest Group on Computational Phonology at HLT-NAACL 2006, pages 32–40,
New York City, USA, June 2006.

their length is lesser than that of the morphemes they replace. Following information-theoretic principles (Shannon, 1948), the length of a pointer to a morpheme (under some optimal encoding scheme) is equal to -1 times the binary logarithm of that morpheme's probability. The length of a signature is the sum of the lengths of the two lists it contains, and the length of each list is the sum of the lengths of the pointers it contains (plus a small cost for the list itself).

This work and related approaches to unsupervised language learning have assumed that there is only one way in which items could be pointed to, or identified. The purpose of this paper is to describe, compare and evaluate several different methods, each of which satisfies MDL's basic requirements, but which have different consequences for the treatment of linguistic phenomena. One the one hand, we contrast the expected description length of "standard" lists of pointers with *polarized* lists of pointers, which are specified as either (i) pointing to the relevant morphemes (those that belong to a signature, or undergo a morpho-phonological rule, for instance) or (ii) pointing to their complement (those that do not belong to a signature, or do not undergo a rule). On the other hand, we compare (polarized) lists of pointers with a method based on binary strings specifying each morpheme as relevant or not (for a given signature, rule, etc.). In particular, we discuss the conditions under which these different ways of pointing are expected to yield more compact descriptions of the data.

The remainder of this paper is organized as follows. In the next section, we give a formal review of the standard treatment of lists of pointers as described in (Goldsmith, 2001); then we successively introduce polarized lists of pointers and the method of binary strings, and make a first, theoretical comparison of them. Section three is devoted to an empirical comparison of these methods on a large natural language corpus. In conclusion, we discuss the implications of our results in the broader context of unsupervised language learning.

2 Variant definitions of pointers

In order to simplify the following theoretical discussion, we temporarily abstract away from the complexity of a full-blown model of morphology. Given a set of N stems and their distribution, we consider the general problem of pointing to a subset of M stems (with $0 < M \leq N$), first by means of "standard" lists of pointers, then by means of polarized ones, and finally by means of binary strings.

2.1 Expected length of lists of pointers

Let τ denote a set of N stems; we assume that the length of a pointer to a specific stem $t \in \tau$ is its inverse log probability $-\log pr(t)$.[2] Now, let $\{M\}$ denote the set of all subsets of τ that contain exactly $0 < M \leq N$ stems. The *description length* of a list of pointers to a particular subset $\mu \in \{M\}$ is defined as the sum of the lengths of the M pointers it contains, plus a small cost of for specifying the list structure itself, defined as $\lambda(M) := 0$ if $M = 0$ and $\log M$ bits otherwise[3]:

$$DL^{\text{ptr}}(\mu) := \lambda(M) - \sum_{t \in \mu} \log pr(t)$$

The *expected* length of a pointer is equal to the entropy over the distribution of stems:

$$h^{\text{stems}} := E_{t \in \tau}[-\log pr(t)] = -\sum_{t \in \tau} pr(t) \log pr(t)$$

Thus, the expected description length of a list of pointers to M stems (over all subsets $\mu \in \{M\}$) is:

$$\begin{aligned} E_{\mu \in \{M\}}[DL^{\text{ptr}}(\mu)] &= \frac{1}{|\{M\}|} \sum_{\mu \in \{M\}} DL^{\text{ptr}}(\mu) \\ &= \lambda(M) + M h^{\text{stems}} \end{aligned} \quad (1)$$

This value increases as a function of both the number of stems which are pointed to and the entropy over the distribution of stems. Since $0 \leq h^{\text{stems}} \leq \log N$, the following bounds hold:

$$\begin{aligned} 0 \leq h^{\text{stems}} &\leq E_{\mu \in \{M\}}[DL^{\text{ptr}}(\mu)] \\ &\leq \log N + N h^{\text{stems}} \leq (N+1) \log N \end{aligned}$$

[2] Here and throughout the paper, we use the notation $\log x$ to refer to the *binary* logarithm of x; thus entropy and other information-theoretic quantities are expressed in terms of *bits*.

[3] Cases where the argument of this function can have the value 0 will arise in the next section.

2.2 Polarization

Consider a set of $N = 3$ equiprobable stems, and suppose that we need to specify that a given morpho-phonological rule applies to one of them. In this context, a list with a single pointer to a stem requires $\log 1 - \log \frac{1}{3} = 1.58$ bits. Suppose now that the rule is more general and applies to two of the three stems. The length of the new list of pointers is thus $\log 2 - 2 \log \frac{1}{3} = 4.17$ bits. It appears that for such a general rule, it is more compact to list the stems to which it does *not* apply, and mark the list with a flag that indicates the "negative" meaning of the pointers. Since the flag signals a binary choice (either the list points to stems that undergo the rule, or to those that do not), $\log 2 = 1$ bit suffices to encode it, so that the length of the new list is $1.58 + 1 = 2.58$ bits.

We propose to use the term *polarized* to refer to lists of pointers bearing a such flag. If it is useful to distinguish between specific settings of the flag, we may speak of *positive* versus *negative* lists of pointers (the latter being the case of our last example). The expected description length of a polarized list of M pointers is:

$$E_{\mu \in \{M\}}\left[DL^{\text{pol}}(\mu)\right] = 1 + \lambda(\hat{M}) + \hat{M} h^{\text{stems}} \quad \text{with } \hat{M} := \min(M, N - M) \tag{2}$$

From (1) and (2), we find that in general, the expected *gain* in description length by polarizing a list of M pointers is:

$$E_{\mu \in \{M\}}\left[DL^{\text{ptr}}(\mu) - DL^{\text{pol}}(\mu)\right] = \begin{cases} -1 \text{ iff } M \leq \frac{N}{2} \\ -1 + \lambda(M) - \lambda(N - M) + (2M - N)h^{\text{stems}} \\ \quad \text{otherwise} \end{cases}$$

Thus, if the number of stems pointed to is lesser than or equal to half the total number of stems, using a polarized list rather than a non-polarized one means wasting exactly 1 bit for encoding the superfluous flag. If the number of stems pointed to is larger than that, we still pay 1 bit for the flag, but the reduced number of pointers results in an expected saving of $\lambda(M) - \lambda(N - M)$ bits for the list structure, plus $(2M - N) \cdot h^{\text{stems}}$ bits for the pointers themselves.

Now, let us assume that we have no information regarding the number M of elements which are pointed to, i.e. that it has a uniform distribution between 1 and N ($M \sim U[1, N]$). Let us further assume that stems follow a Zipfian distribution of parameter s, so that the probability of the k-th most frequent stem is defined as:

$$f(k, N, s) := \frac{1/k^s}{H_{N,s}} \quad \text{with } H_{N,s} := \sum_{n=1}^{N} 1/n^s$$

where $H_{N,s}$ stands for the *harmonic number* of order N of s. The entropy over this distribution is:

$$h_{N,s}^{\text{Zipf}} := \frac{s}{H_{N,s}} \sum_{k=1}^{N} \frac{\log k}{k^s} + \log H_{N,s}$$

Armed with these assumptions, we may now *compute* the expected description length gain of polarization (over all values of M) as a function of N and s:

$$E_M\left(E_{\mu \in \{M\}}\left[DL^{\text{ptr}}(\mu) - DL^{\text{pol}}(\mu)\right]\right) = -1 + \frac{1}{N} \sum_{M=1}^{N} \lambda(M) - \lambda(\hat{M}) + (M - \hat{M}) h_{N,s}^{\text{Zipf}}$$

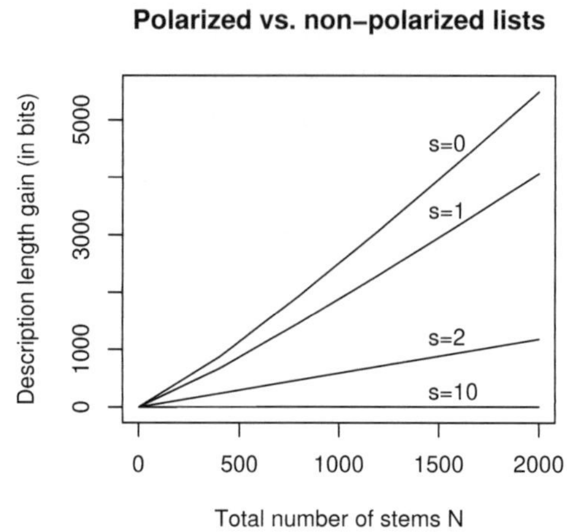

Figure 1: Expected gain in description length by using polarized rather than non-polarized lists of pointers.

Figure 1 shows the gain calculated for N = 1, 400, 800, 1200, 1600 and 2000, and s = 0, 1, 2 and 10. In general, it increases with N, with a slope that depends on s: the greater the value of s, the lesser the entropy over the distribution of stems; since the entropy corresponds to the expected length

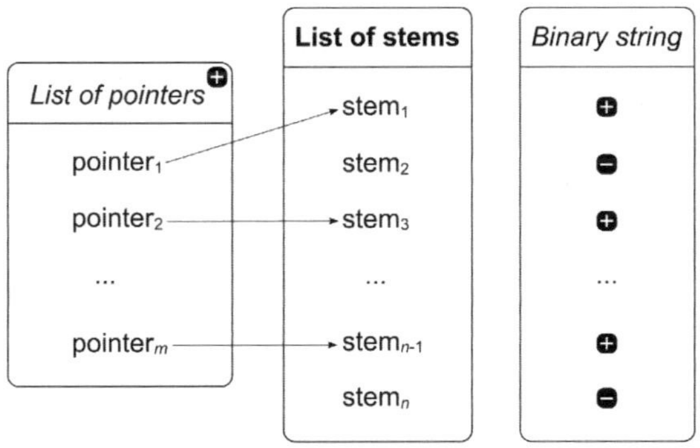

Figure 2: Two ways of pointings to stems: by means of a polarized list of pointers, or a binary string.

of a pointer, its decrease entails a decrease in the number of bits that can be saved by using polarized lists (which generally use less pointers). However, even for an aberrantly skewed distribution of stems[4], the expected gain of polarization remains positive. Since the value of s is usually taken to be slightly greater than 1 for natural languages (Mandelbrot, 1953), it seems that polarized lists generally entail a considerable gain in description length.

2.3 Binary strings

Consider again the problem of pointing to one out of three equiprobable stems. Suppose that the list of stems is ordered, and that we want to point to the first one, for instance. An alternative to the recourse to a list of pointers consists in using a binary string (in this case `100`) where the i-th symbol is set to `1` (or +) if the i-th stem is being pointed to, and to `0` (or −) otherwise. Figure 2 gives a schematic view of these two ways of pointing to items.

There are two main differences between this method and the previous one. On the one hand, the number of symbols in the string is constant and equal to the *total* number N of stems, regardless of the number M of stems that are pointed to. On the other hand, the compressed length of the string depends on the distribution of symbols in it, and *not* on the distribution of stems. Thus, by comparison with the description length of a list of pointers, there is a loss due to the larger number of encoded symbols, and a gain due to the use of an encoding specifically tailored for the relevant distribution of pointed versus "unpointed" elements.

[4]In the case $s = 10$, the probability of the most frequent stem is .999 for $N = 2000$.

The entropy associated with a binary string is entirely determined by the number of `1`'s it contains, i.e. the number M of stems which are pointed to, and the length N of the string:

$$h^{\text{bin}}_{N,M} := -\frac{M}{N}\log\frac{M}{N} - \frac{N-M}{N}\log\frac{N-M}{N}$$

The compressed length of a binary string pointing to M stems is thus:

$$DL^{\text{bin}}(M) := Nh^{\text{bin}}_{N,M} \tag{3}$$

It is maximal and equal to N bits when $M = \frac{N}{2}$, and minimal and equal to 0 when $M = N$, i.e. when *all* stems have a pointer on them. Notice that binary strings are intrinsically polarized, so that interverting `0`'s and `1`'s results in the same description length regardless of their distribution.[5]

The question naturally arises, under which conditions would binary strings be more or less compact than polarized lists of pointers. If we assume again that the distribution of the number of elements pointed to is uniform and the distribution of stems is Zipfian of parameter s, (2) and (3) justify the following expression for the expected description length gain by using binary strings rather than polarized lists (as a function of N and s):

$$E_M\left[E_{\mu\in\{M\}}[DL^{\text{pol}}(\mu)] - DL^{\text{bin}}(M)\right]$$
$$= 1 + \tfrac{1}{N}\sum_{\hat{M}=1}^{N}\lambda(\hat{M}) + \hat{M}h^{\text{Zipf}}_{N,s} - Nh^{\text{bin}}_{N,M}$$

Figure 3 shows the gain calculated for N = 1, 400, 800, 1200, 1600 and 2000, and s = 0, 1, 2 and 3. For s small, i.e. when the entropy over the distribution of stems is greater or not much lesser than that of natural languages, the description length of binary strings is considerably lesser than that of polarized lists. The difference decreases as s increases,

[5]As one the reviewers has indicated to us, the binary strings approach is actually very similar to the method of *combinatorial codes* described by (Rissanen, 1989). This method consists in pointing to one among $\binom{N}{M}$ possible combinations of M stems out of N. Under the assumption that these combinations have a uniform probability, the cost for pointing to M stems is $\log\binom{N}{M}$ bits, which is in general slightly lesser than the description length of the corresponding binary string (the difference being maximal for $M = N/2$, i.e. when the binary string encoding cannot take advantage of any compression).

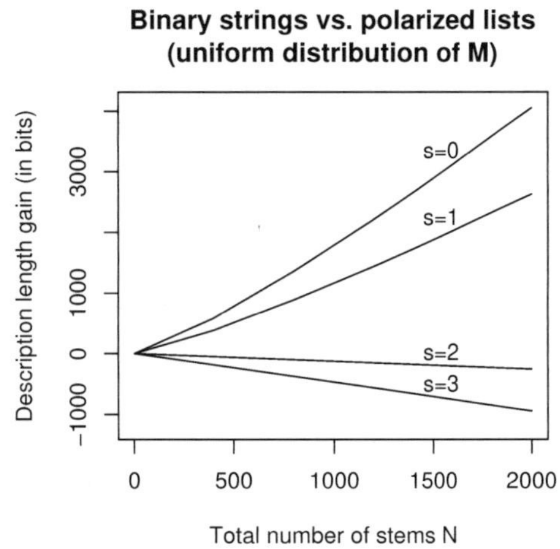

Figure 3: Expected gain in description length by using binary strings rather than polarized lists under the assumption that $M \sim U[1, N]$.

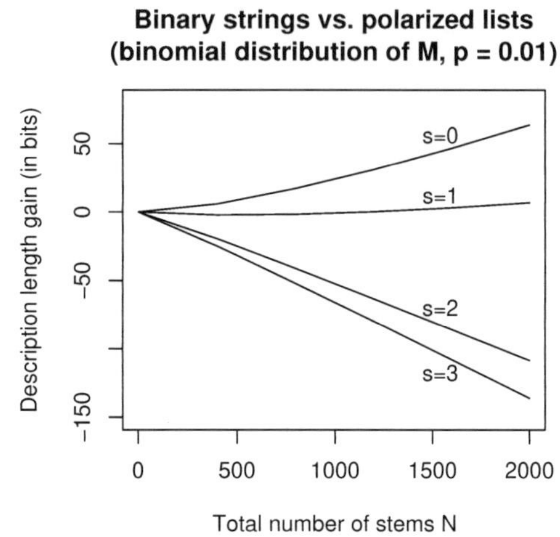

Figure 4: Expected gain in description length by using binary strings rather than polarized lists under the assumption that $M \sim B[N, 0.01]$.

until at some point (around $s = 2$), the situation reverses and polarized lists become more compact. In both cases, the trend increases with the number N of stems (within the range of values observed).

By contrast, it is instructive to consider a case where the distribution of the number of elements pointed to departs from uniformity. For instance, we can make the assumption that M follows a binomial distribution ($M \sim B[N, p]$).[6] Under this assumption (and, as always, that of a Zipfian distribution of stems), the expected description length gain by using binary strings rather than polarized lists is:

$$E_M\big[E_{\mu\in\{M\}}[DL^{\text{ptr}}(\mu)]-DL^{\text{bin}}(M)\big]$$
$$= \textstyle\sum_{M=1}^{N} pr(M)\Big(1+\lambda(\hat{M})+\hat{M}h^{\text{Zipf}}_{N,s}-Nh^{\text{bin}}_{N,M}\Big)$$
$$\text{with } pr(M) = \tbinom{N}{M}p^{M}(1-p)^{N-M}$$

Letting N and s vary as in the previous computation, we set the probability for a stem to have a pointer on it to $p = 0.01$, so that the distribution of pointed versus "unpointed" elements is considerably skewed.[7]

[6] This model predicts that most of the time, the number M of elements pointed to is equal to $N \cdot p$ (where p denotes the probability for a stem to have a pointer on it), and that the probability $pr(M)$ of other values of M decreases as they diverge from $N \cdot p$.

[7] By symmetry, the same results would be found with $p = 0.99$.

As shown on figure 4, under these conditions, the absolute value of the gain of using binary strings gets much smaller in general, and the value of s for which the gain becomes negative for N large gets close to 1 (for this particular value, it becomes positive at some point between $N = 1200$ and $N = 1600$).

Altogether, under the assumptions that we have used, these theoretical considerations suggest that binary strings generally yield shorter description lengths than polarized lists of pointers. Of course, data for which these assumptions do not hold could arise. In the perspective of unsupervised learning, it would be particularily interesting to observe that such data drive the learner to induce a different model depending on the representation of pointers being adopted.

It should be noted that nothing prevents binary strings and lists of pointers from coexisting in a single system, which would select the most compact one for each particular case. On the other hand, it is a logical necessity that all lists of pointers be of the same kind, either polarized or not.

3 Experiments

In the previous section, by assuming frequencies of stems and possible distributions of M (the number of stems per signature), we have explored theoretically the differences between several encoding

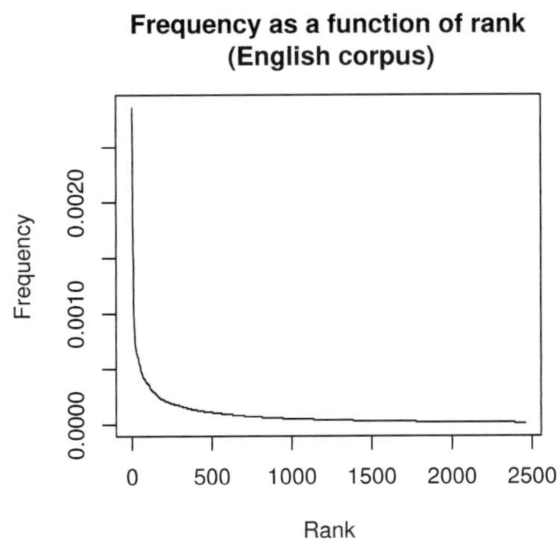

Figure 5: Frequency versus rank (stems) in English corpus.

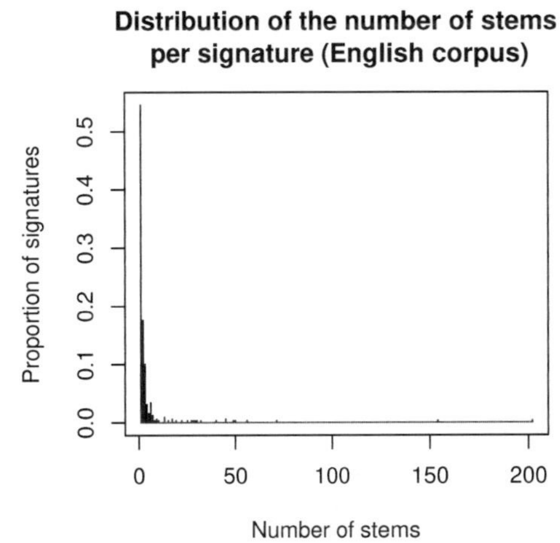

Figure 6: Distribution of number of stems per signature (English corpus)

methods in the MDL framework. In this section, we apply these methods to the problem of suffix discovery in natural language corpora, in order to verify the theoretical predictions we made previously. Thus, the purpose of these experiments is not to state that one encoding is preferable to the others; rather, we want to answer the three following questions:

1. Are our assumptions on the frequency of stems and size of signatures appropriate for natural language corpora?
2. Given these assumptions, do our theoretical analyses correctly predict the difference in description length of two encodings?
3. What is the relationship between the gain in description length and the size of the corpus?

3.1 Experimental methodology

In this experiment, for the purpose of calculating distinct description lengths while using different encoding methods, we modified *Linguistica*[8] by implementing *list of pointers* and *binary strings* as alternative means to encode the pointers from signatures to their associated stems[9]. As a result, given a set of signatures, we are able to compute a description length for each encoding methods.

Within *Linguistica*, the morphology learning process can be divided into a sequence of heuristics, each of which searches for possible incremental modifications to the current morphology. For example, in the suffix-discovery procedure, ten heuristics are carried out successively; thus, we have a distinct set of signatures after applying each of the ten heuristics. Then, for each of these sets, we encode the *pointers* from each signature to its corresponding stems in three rival ways: as a *list of pointers* (polarized or not), as traditionally understood, and as a *binary string*. This way, we can compute the total description length of the signature-stem-linkage for each of the ten sets of signatures and for each of three two ways of encoding the pointers. We also collect statistics on word frequencies and on the distribution of the size of signatures M, i.e. the number M of stems which are are pointed to, both of which are important parametric components in our theoretical analysis.

Experiments are carried out on two orthographic corpora (English and French), each of which has 100,000 word tokens.

3.2 Frequency of stems and size of signatures

The frequency of stems as a function of their rank and the distribution of the size of signatures are plot-

[8]The source and binary files can be freely downloaded at `http://linguistica.uchicago.edu`.

[9]Pointers to *suffixes* are not considered here.

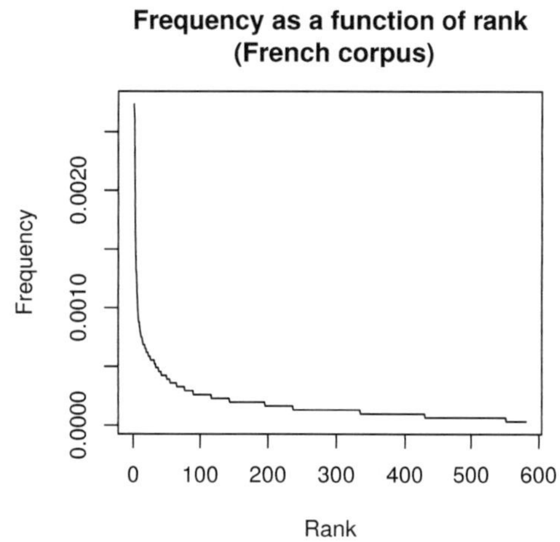

Figure 7: Frequency versus rank (stems) in French corpus.

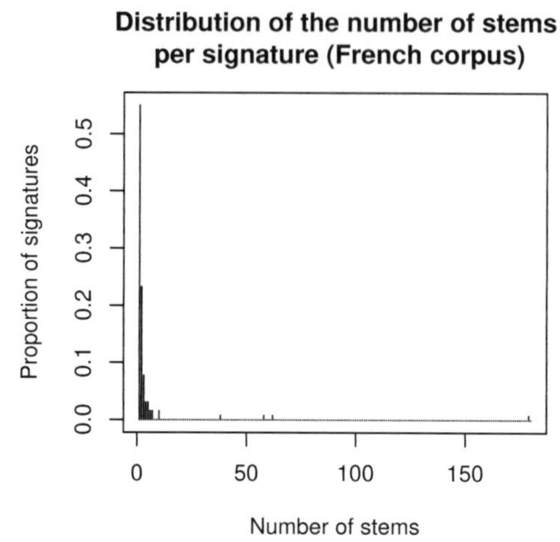

Figure 8: Distribution of number of stems per signature (French corpus)

ted in figures 5 and 6 for the English corpus, and in figures 7 and 8 for the French corpus. These graphs show that in both the English and the French corpora, stems appear to have a distribution similar to a Zipfian one. In addition, in both corpora, M follows a distribution whose character we are not sure of, but which appears more similar to a binomial distribution. To some extent, these observations are consistent with the assumptions we made in the previous theoretical analysis.

3.3 Description length of each encoding

The description length obtained with each encoding method is displayed in figures 9 (English corpus) and 10 (French corpus), in which the x-axis refers to the set of signatures resulting from the application of each successive heuristics, and the y-axis corresponds to the description length in bits. Note that we only plot description lengths of *non-polarized* lists of pointers, because the number of stems per signature is always less than half the total number of stems in these data (and we expect that this would be true for other languages as well).[10]

These two plots show that in both corpora, there is always a gain in description length by using binary strings rather than lists of pointers for encoding the pointers from signatures to stems. This observation is consistent with our conclusion in section 2.3, but it is important to emphasize again that for other data (or other applications), lists of pointers might turn out to be more compact.

3.4 Description length gain as a function of corpus size

In order to evaluate the effect of corpus size on the gain in description length by using binary string rather than lists of variable-length pointers, we applied *Linguistica* to a number of English corpora of different sizes ranging between 5,000 to 200,000 tokens. For the final set of signatures obtained with each corpus, we then compute the gain of binary strings encoding over lists of pointers as we did in the previous experiments. The results are plotted in figure 11.

This graph shows a strong positive correlation between description length gain and corpus size. This is reminiscent of the results of our theoretical simulations displayed in figures 3 and 4. As before, we interpret the match between the experimental results and the theoretical expectations as evidence supporting the validity of our theoretical predictions.

3.5 Discussion of experiments

These experiments are actually a number of case studies, in which we verify the applicability of our theoretical analysis on variant definitions of pointer lengths in the MDL framework. For the particu-

[10] See figures 6 and 8 as well as section 2.2 above.

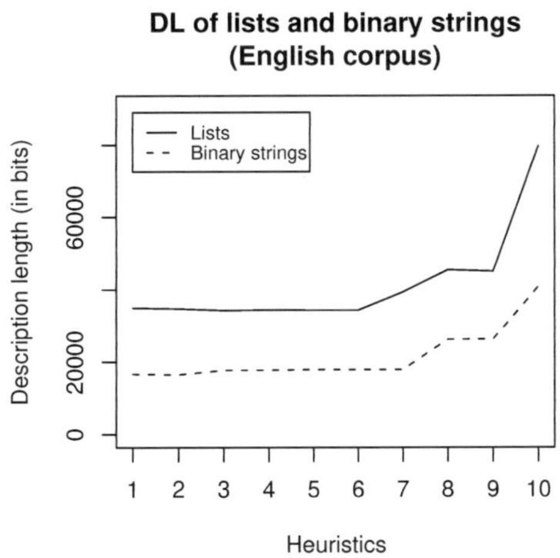

Figure 9: Comparison of DL of 10 successive morphologies using pointers versus binary strings (English corpus).

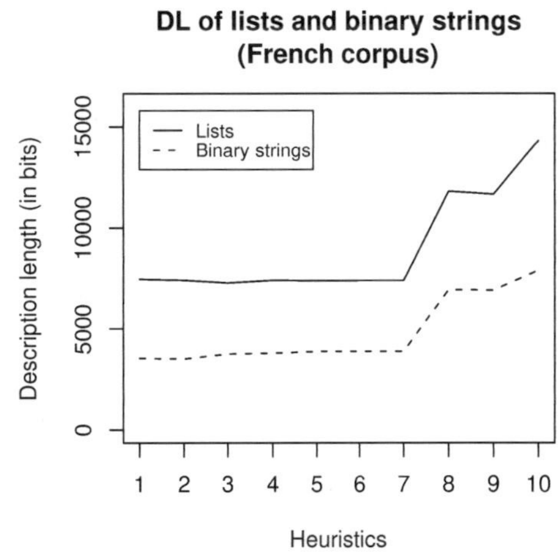

Figure 10: Comparison of DL of 10 successive morphologies using pointers versus binary strings (French corpus)

lar application we considered, learning morphology with *Linguistica*, binary strings encoding proves to be more compact than lists of variable-length pointers. However, the purpose of this paper is not to predict that one variant is always better, but rather to explore the mathematics behind different encodings. Armed with the mathematical analysis of different encodings, we hope to be better capable of making the right choice under specific conditions. In particular, in the suffix-discovery application (and for the languages we examined), our results are consistent with the assumptions we made and the predictions we derived from them.

4 Conclusion

The overall purpose of this paper has been to illustrate what was for us an unexpected aspect of using Minimum Description Length theory: not only does MDL not specify the form of a grammar (or morphology), but it does not even specify the precise form in which the description of the abstract linkages between concepts (such as stems and signatures) should be encoded and quantitatively evaluated. We have seen that in a range of cases, using binary strings instead of the more traditional frequency-based pointers leads to a smaller overall grammar length, and there is no guarantee that we will not find an even shorter way to accomplish the same thing tomorrow[11]. Simply put, MDL is emphatically an evaluation procedure, and not a discovery procedure.

We hope to have shown, as well, that a systematic exploration of the nature of the difference between standard frequency-based pointer lengths and binary string based representations is possible, and we can develop reasonably accurate predictions or expectations as to which type of description will be less costly in any given case.

Acknowledgements

This research was supported by a grant of the Swiss National Science Foundation to the first author.

References

C. de Marcken. 1996. *Unsupervised Language Acquisition*. Ph.D. thesis, MIT, Cambridge, MA.

J. Goldsmith. 2001. The unsupervised learning of natural language morphology. *Computational Linguistics*, 27(2):153–198.

B. Mandelbrot. 1953. An informational theory of the statistical structure of language. In Willis Jackson, editor, *Communication Theory, the Second London Symposium*, pages 486–502. Butterworth: London.

[11] See note 5.

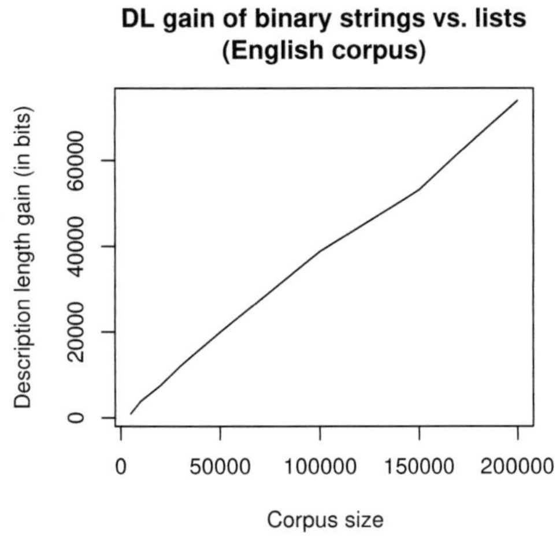

Figure 11: DL gain from using binary string versus size of corpus (English corpus)

J. Rissanen. 1989. *Stochastic Complexity in Statistical Inquiry*. World Scientific Publishing Co, Singapore.

C.E. Shannon. 1948. A mathematical theory of communication. *Bell Systems Technical Journal*, 27:379–423.

Improved morpho-phonological sequence processing with constraint satisfaction inference

Antal van den Bosch and **Sander Canisius**
ILK / Language and Information Science
Tilburg University, P.O. Box 90153, NL-5000 LE Tilburg, The Netherlands
{Antal.vdnBosch,S.V.M.Canisius}@uvt.nl

Abstract

In performing morpho-phonological sequence processing tasks, such as letter-phoneme conversion or morphological analysis, it is typically not enough to base the output sequence on local decisions that map local-context input windows to single output tokens. We present a global sequence-processing method that repairs inconsistent local decisions. The approach is based on local predictions of overlapping trigrams of output tokens, which open up a space of possible sequences; a data-driven constraint satisfaction inference step then searches for the optimal output sequence. We demonstrate significant improvements in terms of word accuracy on English and Dutch letter-phoneme conversion and morphological segmentation, and we provide qualitative analyses of error types prevented by the constraint satisfaction inference method.

1 Introduction

The fields of computational phonology and morphology were among the earlier fields in computational linguistics to adopt machine learning algorithms as a means to automatically construct processing systems from data. For instance, letter-phoneme conversion was already pioneered, with neural networks initially, at the end of the 1980s (Sejnowski and Rosenberg, 1987), and was shortly after also investigated with memory-based learning and analogical approaches (Weijters, 1991; Van den Bosch and Daelemans, 1993; Yvon, 1996) and decision trees (Torkkola, 1993; Dietterich et al., 1995). The development of these data-driven systems was thrusted by the early existence of lexical databases, originally compiled to serve (psycho)linguistic research purposes, such as the CELEX lexical database for Dutch, English, and German (Baayen et al., 1993). Many researchers have continued and are still continuing this line of work, generally producing successful systems with satisfactory, though still imperfect performance.

A key characteristic of many of these early systems is that they perform decomposed or simplified versions of the full task. Rather than predicting the full phonemization of a word given its orthography in one go, the task is decomposed in predicting individual phonemes or subsequences of phonemes. Analogously, rather than generating a full wordform, many morphological generation systems produce transformation codes (e.g., "add -er and umlaut") that need to be applied to the input string by a post-processing automaton. These task simplifications are deliberately chosen to avoid sparseness problems to the machine learning systems. Such systems tend to perform badly when there are many low-frequent and too case-specific classes; task decomposition allows them to be robust and generic when they process unseen words.

This task decomposition strategy has a severe drawback in sequence processing tasks. Decomposed systems do not have any global method to check whether their local decisions form a globally

Proceedings of the Eighth Meeting of the ACL Special Interest Group on Computational Phonology at HLT-NAACL 2006, pages 41–49,
New York City, USA, June 2006.

coherent output. If a letter-phoneme conversion system predicts schwas on every vowel in a polysyllabic word such as *parameter* because it is uncertain about the ambiguous mapping of each of the *a*s and *e*s, it produces a bad pronunciation. Likewise, if a morphological analysis system segments a word such as *being* as a prefix followed by an inflection, making the locally most likely guesses, it generates an analysis that could never exist, since it lacks a stem.

Global models that coordinate, mediate, or enforce that the output is a valid sequence are typically formulated in the form of linguistic rules, applied during processing or in post-processing, that constrain the space of possible output sequences. Some present-day research in machine learning of morpho-phonology indeed focuses on satisfying linguistically-motivated constraints as a post-processing or filtering step; e.g., see (Daya et al., 2004) on identifying roots in Hebrew word forms. Optimality Theory (Prince and Smolensky, 2004) can also be seen as a constraint-based approach to language processing based on linguistically motivated constraints. In contrast to being motivated by linguistic theory, constraints in a global model can be learned automatically from data as well. In this paper we propose such a data-driven constraint satisfaction inference method, that finds a globally appropriate output sequence on the basis of a space of possible sequences generated by a locally-operating classifier predicting output subsequences. We show that the method significantly improves on the basic method of predicting single output tokens at a time, on English and Dutch letter-phoneme conversion and morphological analysis.

This paper is structured as follows. The constraint satisfaction inference method is outlined in Section 2. We describe the four morpho-phonological processing tasks, and the lexical data from which we extracted examples for these tasks, in Section 3. We subsequently list the outcomes of the experiments in Section 4, and conclude with a discussion of our findings in Section 5.

2 Class trigrams and constraint satisfaction inference

Both the letter-phoneme conversion and the morphological analysis tasks treated in this paper can be seen as sequentially-structured classification tasks, where sequences of letters are mapped to sequences of phonemes or morphemes. Such sequence-to-sequence mappings are a frequently reoccurring phenomenon in natural language processing, which suggests that it is preferable to take care of the issue of classifying sequential data once at the machine learning level, rather than repeatedly and in different ways at the level of practical applications. Recently, a machine learning approach for sequential data has been proposed by Van den Bosch and Daelemans (2005) that is suited for discrete machine-learning algorithms such as memory-based learners, which have been shown to perform well on word phonemization and morphological analysis before (Van den Bosch and Daelemans, 1993; Van den Bosch and Daelemans, 1999). In the remainder of this paper, we use as our classifier of choice the IB1 algorithm (Aha et al., 1991) with feature weighting, as implemented in the TiMBL software package[1] (Daelemans et al., 2004).

In the approach to sequence processing proposed by Van den Bosch and Daelemans (2005), the elements of the input sequence (in the remainder of this paper, we will refer to words and letters rather than the more general terms sequences and sequence elements) are assigned overlapping subsequences of output symbols. This subsequence corresponds to the output symbols for a *focus* letter, and one letter to its left and one letter to its right. Predicting such trigram subsequences for each letter of a word eventually results in three output symbol predictions for each letter. In many cases, those three predictions will not agree, resulting in a number of potential output sequences. We will refer to the procedure for selecting the final output sequence from the space of alternatives spanned by the predicted trigrams as an inference procedure, analogously to the use of this term in probabilistic sequence classification methods (Punyakanok and Roth, 2001). The original work on predicting class trigrams implemented a simple inference procedure by voting over the three predicted symbols (Van den Bosch and Daelemans, 2005).

Predicting trigrams of overlapping output symbols has been shown to be an effective approach

[1]TiMBL URL: http://ilk.uvt.nl/timbl/

to improve sequence-oriented natural language processing tasks such as syntactic chunking and named-entity recognition, where an input sequence of tokens is mapped to an output sequence of symbols encoding a syntactic or semantic segmentation of the sentence. Letter-phoneme conversion and morphological analysis, though sequentially structured on another linguistic level, may be susceptible to benefiting from this approach as well.

In addition to the practical improvement shown to be obtained with the class trigram method, there is also a more theoretical attractiveness to it. Since the overlapping trigrams that are predicted are just atomic symbols to the underlying learning algorithm, a classifier will only predict output symbol trigrams that are actually present in the data it was trained on. Consequently, predicted trigrams are guaranteed to be syntactically valid subsequences in the target task. There is no such guarantee in approaches to sequence classification where an isolated local classifier predicts single output symbols at a time, without taking into account predictions made elsewhere in the word.

While the original voting-based inference procedure proposed by Van den Bosch and Daelemans (2005) manages to exploit the sequential information stored in the predicted trigrams to improve upon the performance of approaches that do not consider the sequential structure of their output at all, it does so only partly. Essentially, the voting-based inference procedure just splits the overlapping trigrams into their unigram components, thereby retaining only the overlapping symbols for each individual letter. As a result, the guaranteed validity of the trigram subsequences is not put to use. In this section we describe an alternative inference procedure, based on principles of constraint satisfaction, that does manage to use the sequential information provided by the trigram predictions.

At the foundation of this constraint-satisfaction-based inference procedure, more briefly constraint satisfaction inference, is the assumption that the output symbol sequence should preferably be constructed by concatenating the predicted trigrams of output symbols, rather than by chaining individual symbols. However, as the underlying base classifier is by no means perfect, predicted trigrams should not be copied blindly to the output sequence; they may be incorrect. If a trigram prediction is considered to be of insufficient quality, the procedure backs off to symbol bigrams or even symbol unigrams.

The intuitive description of the inference procedure is formalized by expressing it as a weighted constraint satisfaction problem (W-CSP). Constraint satisfaction is a well-studied research area with many diverse areas of application. Weighted constraint satisfaction extends the traditional constraint satisfaction framework with soft constraints; such constraints are not required to be satisfied for a solution to be valid, but constraints a given solution does satisfy are rewarded according to weights assigned to them. Soft constraints are perfect for expressing our preference for symbol trigrams, with the possibility of a back off to lower-degree n-grams if there is reason to doubt the quality of the trigram predictions.

Formally, a W-CSP is a tuple (X, D, C, W). Here, $X = \{x_1, x_2, \ldots, x_n\}$ is a finite set of variables. $D(x)$ is a function that maps each variable to its domain, that is, the set of values that variable can take on. C is the set of constraints. While a variable's domain dictates the values a single variable is allowed to take on, a constraint specifies which simultaneous value *combinations* over a number of variables are allowed. For a traditional (non-weighted) constraint satisfaction problem, a valid solution would be an assignment of values to the variables that (1) are a member of the corresponding variable's domain, and (2) satisfy *all* constraints in the set C. Weighted constraint satisfaction, however, relaxes this requirement to satisfy all constraints. Instead, constraints are assigned weights that may be interpreted as reflecting the importance of satisfying that constraint.

Let a constraint $c \in C$ be defined as a function that maps each variable assignment to 1 if the constraint is satisfied, or to 0 if it is not. In addition, let $W\colon C \rightarrow \mathbb{R}^+$ denote a function that maps each constraint to a positive real value, reflecting the weight of that constraint. Then, the optimal solution to a W-CSP is given by the following equation.

$$\mathbf{x}^* = \arg\max_{\mathbf{x}} \sum_{c} W(c)c(\mathbf{x})$$

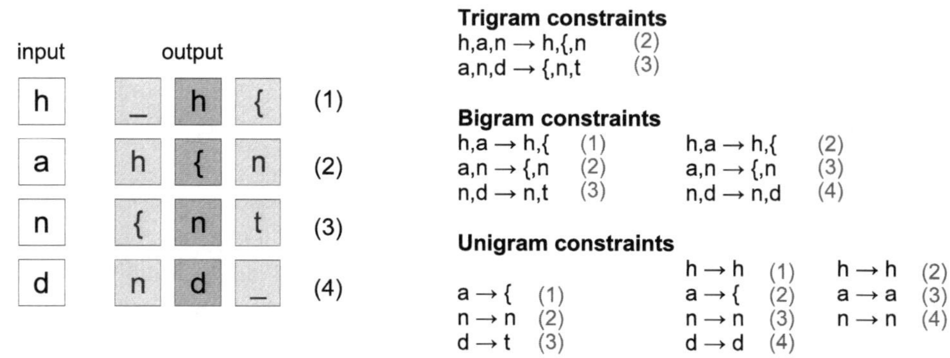

Figure 1: Illustration of the constraints yielded by a given sequence of predicted class trigrams for the word *hand*. The constraints on the right have been marked with a number (between parentheses) that refers to the trigram prediction on the left from which the constraint was derived.

That is, the assignment of values to its variables that maximizes the sum of weights of the constraints that have been satisfied.

Translating the terminology used in morphophonological tasks to the constraint satisfaction domain, each letter maps to a variable, the domain of which corresponds to the three overlapping candidate symbols for this letter suggested by the trigrams covering the letter. This provides us with a definition of the function D, mapping variables to their domain. In the following, $y_{i,j}$ denotes the candidate symbol for letter x_j predicted by the trigram assigned to letter x_i.

$$D(x_i) = \{y_{i-1,i}, y_{i,i}, y_{i+1,i}\}$$

Constraints are extracted from the predicted trigrams. Given the goal of retaining predicted trigrams in the output symbol sequence as much as possible, the most important constraints are simply the trigrams themselves. A predicted trigram describes a subsequence of length three of the entire output sequence; by turning such a trigram into a constraint, we express the wish to have this trigram end up in the final output sequence.

$$(x_{i-1}, x_i, x_{i+1}) = (y_{i,i-1}, y_{i,i}, y_{i,i+1}), \forall i$$

No base classifier is flawless though, and therefore not all predicted trigrams can be expected to be correct. Yet, even an incorrect trigram may carry some useful information regarding the output sequence: one trigram also covers two bigrams, and three unigrams. An incorrect trigram may still contain smaller subsequences of length one or two that are correct. Therefore, all of these are also mapped to constraints.

$$\begin{aligned} (x_{i-1}, x_i) &= (y_{i,i-1}, y_{i,i}), & \forall i \\ (x_i, x_{i+1}) &= (y_{i,i}, y_{i,i+1}), & \forall i \end{aligned}$$

$$\begin{aligned} x_{i-1} &= y_{i,i-1}, & \forall i \\ x_i &= y_{i,i}, & \forall i \\ x_{i+1} &= y_{i,i+1}, & \forall i \end{aligned}$$

To illustrate the above procedure, Figure 1 shows the constraints yielded by a given output sequence of class trigrams for the word "hand". With such an amount of overlapping constraints, the satisfaction problem obtained easily becomes over-constrained, that is, no variable assignment exists that can satisfy all constraints without breaking another. Even only one incorrectly predicted class trigram already leads to two conflicting candidate symbols for one of the letters at least. In Figure 1, this is the case for the letter "d", for which both the symbol "d" and "t" are predicted. On the other hand, without conflicting candidate symbols, no inference would be needed to start with. The choice for the weighted constraint satisfaction method always allows a solution to be found, even in the presence of conflicting constraints. Rather than requiring all constraints to be satisfied, each constraint is assigned a certain weight; the optimal solution to the problem is an assignment of values to the variables that optimizes the

Left context			Focus letter	Right context			Trigram output classes	
							Phonemization	Morph. analysis
_	_	_	b	o	o	k	_bu	_s-
_	_	b	o	o	k	i	bu-	s--
_	b	o	o	k	i	n	u-k	---
b	o	o	k	i	n	g	-kI	--i
o	o	k	i	n	g	_	kIN	-i-
o	k	i	n	g	_	_	IN-	i--
k	i	n	g	_	_	_	N-_	--_

Table 1: Seven labeled examples of phonemization and morphological analysis trigram mappings created for the word *booking*.

sum of weights of the constraints that are satisfied.

As weighted constraints are defined over overlapping subsequences of the output sequence, the best symbol assignment for each letter with respect to the weights of satisfied constraints is decided upon on a global sequence level. This may imply taking into account symbol assignments for surrounding letters to select the best output symbol for a certain letter. In contrast, in non-global approaches, ignorant of any sequential context, only the local classifier prediction with highest confidence is considered for selecting a letter's output symbol. By formulating our inference procedure as a constraint satisfaction problem, global output optimization comes for free: in constraint satisfaction, the aim is also to find a globally optimal assignment of variables taking into account all constraints defined over them. Yet, for such a constraint satisfaction formulation to be effective, good constraint weights should be chosen, that is, weights that favor good output sequences over bad ones.

Constraints can directly be traced back to a prediction made by the base classifier. If two constraints are in conflict, the one which the classifier was most certain of should preferably be satisfied. In the W-CSP framework, this preference can be expressed by weighting constraints according to the classifier confidence for the originating trigram. For the memory-based learner, we define the classifier confidence for a predicted class as the weight assigned to that class in the neighborhood of the test instance, divided by the total weight of all classes.

Let x denote a test instance, and c^* its predicted class. Constraints derived from this class are weighted according to the following rules:

- for a trigram constraint, the weight is simply the base classifier's confidence value for the class c^*;
- for a bigram constraint, the weight is the sum of the confidences for all trigram classes in the nearest-neighbor set of x that assign the same symbol bigram to the letters spanned by the constraint;
- for a unigram constraint, the weight is the sum of the confidences for all trigram classes in the nearest-neighbor set of x that assign the same symbol to the letter spanned by the constraint.

This weighting scheme results in an inference procedure that behaves exactly as we already described intuitively in the beginning of this section. The preference for retaining the predicted trigrams in the output sequence is translated into high rewards for output sequences that do so, since such output sequences not only receive credit for the satisfied trigram constraints, but also for all the bigram and unigram constraints derived from that trigram; they are necessarily satisfied as well. Nonetheless, this preference for trigrams may be abandoned if composing a certain part of the output sequence from several symbol bigrams or even unigrams results in higher rewards than when trigrams are used. The latter may happen in cases where the base classifier is not confident about its trigram predictions.

3 Data preparation

In our experiments we train classifiers on English and Dutch letter-phoneme conversion and morphological analysis. All data for the experiments described in this paper are extracted from the CELEX lexical databases for English and Dutch (Baayen et al., 1993). We encode the examples for our base classifiers in a uniform way, along the following procedure. Given a word and (i) an aligned phonemic transcription or (ii) an aligned encoding of a morphological analysis, we generate letter-by-letter windows. Each window takes one letter in focus, and includes three neighboring letters to the left and to the right. Each seven-letter input window is associated to a trigram class label, composed of the focus class label aligned with the middle letter, plus its immediately preceding and following class labels. Table 1 displays the seven examples made on the basis of the word *booking*, with trigram classes (as explained in Section 2) both for the letter-phoneme conversion task and for the morphological analysis task. The full aligned phonemic transcription of *booking* is [bu-kIN-] (using the SAMPA coding of the international phonetic alphabet), and the morphological analysis of *booking* is $[book]_{stem}[\text{ing}]_{inflection}$. The dashes in the phonemic transcription are inserted to ensure a one-to-one mapping between letters and phonemes; the insertion was done by automatical alignment through expectation-maximization (Dempster et al., 1977).

The English word phonemization data, extracted from the CELEX lexical database, contains 65,467 words, on the basis of which we create a database of 573,170 examples. The Dutch word phonemization data set consists of 293,825 words, totaling to 3,181,345 examples. Both data sets were aligned using the expectation-maximization algorithm (Dempster et al., 1977), using a phonemic null character to equalize the number of symbols in cases in which the phonemic transcription is shorter than the orthographic word, and using "double phonemes" (e.g. [X] for [ks]) in cases where the phonemic transcription is longer, as in *taxi* – [tAksi].

CELEX contains 336,698 morphological analyses of Dutch (which we converted to 3,209,090 examples), and 65,558 analyses of English words (573,544 examples). We converted the available

Left context			Focus letter	Right context			Trigram class
_	_	_	a	b	n	o	_ A 0
_	_	a	b	n	o	r	A 0 0
_	a	b	n	o	r	m	0 0 0
a	b	n	o	r	m	a	0 0 0
b	n	o	r	m	a	l	0 0 0
n	o	r	m	a	l	i	0 0 0
o	r	m	a	l	i	t	0 0 0+Da
r	m	a	l	i	t	e	0 0+Da A_→N
m	a	l	i	t	e	i	0+Da A_→N 0
a	l	i	t	e	i	t	A_→N 0 0
l	i	t	e	i	t	e	0 0 0
i	t	e	i	t	e	n	0 0 0
t	e	i	t	e	n	_	0 0 plural
e	i	t	e	n	_	_	0 plural 0
i	t	e	n	_	_	_	plural 0 _

Table 2: Examples with morphological analysis trigram classes derived from the example word *abnormaliteiten*.

morphological information for the two languages in a coding scheme which is rather straightforward in the case of English, and somewhat more complicated for Dutch. For English, as exemplified in Table 1, a simple segmentation label marks the beginning of either a stem, an inflection ("s" and "i" in Table 1), a stress-affecting affix, or a stress-neutral affix ("1" and "2", not shown in Table 1). The coding scheme for Dutch incorporates additional information on the part-of-speech of every stem and non-inflectional affix, the type of inflection, and also encodes all spelling changes between the base lemma forms and the surface word form.

To illustrate the more complicated construction of examples for Dutch morphological analysis, Table 2 displays the 15 instances derived from the Dutch example word *abnormaliteiten* (abnormalities) and their associated classes. The class of the first instance is A, which signifies that the morpheme starting in *a* is an adjective (A). The class of the eighth instance, 0+Da, indicates that at that position no segment starts (0), but that an *a* was deleted at that position (+Da, "delete a" here). Next to deletions, insertions (+I) and replacements (+R, with a deletion and an insertion argument) can also occur. Together

Language	Task	Unigrams	Trigrams
English	Letter-phon.	58	13,005
	Morphology	5	80
Dutch	Letter-phon.	201	17,538
	Morphology	3,831	14,795

Table 3: Numbers of unigram and trigram classes for the four tasks.

these two classification labels code that the first morpheme is the adjective *abnormaal*. The second morpheme, the suffix *iteit*, has class A_→N. This complex tag, which is in fact a rewrite rule, indicates that when *iteit* attaches right to an adjective (encoded by A_), the new combination becomes a noun (→N). Rewrite rule class labels occur exclusively with suffixes, that do not have a part-of-speech tag of their own, but rather seek an attachment to form a complex morpheme with the part-of-speech tag. Finally, the third morpheme is *en*, which is a plural inflection that by definition attaches to a noun.

Logically, the number of trigram classes for each task is larger than the number of atomic classes; the actual numbers for the four tasks investigated here are displayed in Table 3. The English morphological analysis task has the lowest number of trigram classes, 80, due to the fact that there are only five atomic classes in the original task, but for the other tasks the number of trigram classes is quite high; above 10,000. With these numbers of classes, several machine learning algorithms are practically ruled out, given their high sensitivity to numbers of classes (e.g., support vector machines or rule learners). Memory-based learning algorithms, however, are among a small set of machine learning algorithms that are insensitive to the number of classes both in learning and in classification.

4 Results

We performed experiments with the memory-based learning algorithm IB1, equipped with constraint satisfaction inference post-processing, on the four aforementioned tasks. In one variant, IB1 was simply used to predict atomic classes, while in the other variant IB1 predicted trigram classes, and constraint satisfaction inference was used for post-processing the output sequences. We chose to measure the generalization performance of our trained classifiers on a single 90% training set – 10% test set split of each data set (after shuffling the data randomly at the word level), and measuring the percentage of fully correctly phonemized words or fully correctly morphologically analyzed words – arguably the most critical and unbiased performance metric for both tasks. Additionally we performed bootstrap resampling (Noreen, 1989) to obtain confidence intervals.

Language	Method	Word accuracy
English	Unigram	80.0 ±0.75
	CSInf	85.4 ±0.71
Dutch	Unigram	41.3 ±0.48
	CSInf	51.9 ±0.48

Table 4: Word accuracies on English and Dutch morphological analysis by the default unigram classifier and the trigram method with constraint satisfaction inference, with confidence intervals.

Language	Method	Word accuracy
English	Unigram	79.0 ±0.82
	CSInf	84.5 ±0.76
Dutch	Unigram	92.8 ±0.25
	CSInf	94.4 ±0.22

Table 5: Word accuracies on English and Dutch letter-phoneme conversion by the default unigram classifier and the trigram method with constraint satisfaction inference, with confidence intervals.

Table 4 lists the word accuracies obtained on the English and Dutch morphological analysis tasks. Constraint satisfaction inference significantly outperforms the systems that predict atomic unigram classes, by a large margin. While the absolute differences in scores between the two variants of English morphological analysis is 5.4%, the error reduction is an impressive 27%.

Table 5 displays the word phonemization accuracies of both variants on both languages. Again, significant improvements over the baseline classifier can be observed; the confidence intervals are widely apart. Error reductions for both languages are impressive: 26% for English, and 22% for Dutch.

5 Discussion

We have presented constraint satisfaction inference as a global method to repair errors made by a local classifier. This classifier is a memory-based learner predicting overlapping trigrams, creating a space of possible output sequences in which the inference procedure finds the globally optimal one. This globally optimal sequence is the one that adheres best to the trigram, bigram, and unigram sub-sequence constraints present in the predictions of the local classifier, weighted by the confidences of the classifier, in a back-off order from trigrams to unigrams.

The method is shown to significantly outperform a memory-based classifier predicting atomic classes and lacking any global post-processing, which has previously been shown to exhibit successful performance (Van den Bosch and Daelemans, 1993; Van den Bosch and Daelemans, 1999). (While this was the reason for using memory-based learning, we note that the constraint satisfaction inference and its underlying trigram-based classification method can be applied to any machine-learning classifier.) The large improvements (27% and 26% error reductions on the two English tasks, 18% and 22% on the two Dutch tasks) can arguably be taken as an indication that this method may be quite effective in general in morpho-phonological sequence processing tasks.

Apparently, the constraint-satisfaction method is able to avoid more errors than to add them. At closer inspection, comparing cases in which the atomic classifier generates errors and constraint satisfaction inference does not, we find that the type of avoided error, when compared to the unigram classifier, differs per task. On the morphological analysis task, we identify repairs where (1) a correct segmentation is inserted, (2) a false segmentation is not placed, and (3) a tag is switched. As Table 6 shows in its upper four lines, in the case of English most repairs involve correctly inserted segmentations, but the other two categories are also quite frequent. In the case of Dutch the most common repair is a switch from an incorrect tag, placed at the right segmentation position, to the correct tag at that point. Given that there are over three thousand possible tags in our complicated Dutch morphological analysis task, this is indeed a likely area where there is room for improvement.

Morphological analysis repairs	English	Dutch
Insert segmentation	193	1,087
Delete segmentation	158	1,083
Switch tag	138	2,505
Letter-phoneme repairs	**English**	**Dutch**
Alignment	1,049	239
Correct vowel	32	94
Correct consonant	275	73

Table 6: Numbers of repaired errors divided over three categories of morphological analysis classifications (top) and letter-phoneme conversions (bottom) of the constraint satisfaction inference method as compared to the unigram classifier.

The bottom four lines of Table 6 lists the counts of repaired errors in word phonemization in both languages, where we distinguish between (1) alignment repairs between phonemes and alignment symbols (where phonemes are corrected to phonemic nulls, or vice versa), (2) switches from incorrect non-null phonemes to correct vowels, and (3) switches from incorrect non-null phonemes to correct consonants. Contrary to expectation, it is not the second vowel category in which most repairs are made (many of the vowel errors in fact remain in the output), but the alignment category, in both languages. At points where the local unigram classifier sometimes incorrectly predicts a phoneme twice, where it should have predicted it along with a phonemic null, the constraint satisfaction inference method never generates a double phoneme. Hence, the method succeeds in generating sequences that are *possible*, and avoiding impossible sub-sequences. At the same time, a *possible* sequence is not necessarily the *correct* sequence, so this method can be expected to still make errors on the identity of labels in the output sequence.

In future work we plan to test a range of n-gram widths exceeding the current trigrams. Preliminary results suggest that the method retains a positive effect over the baseline with $n > 3$, but it does not outperform the $n = 3$ case. We also intend to test the method with a range of different machine learning methods, since as we noted before the constraint-satisfaction inference method and its underlying n-gram output subsequence classification method can be applied to any machine learning classification algorithm in principle, as is already supported by preliminary work in this direction.

Also, we plan comparisons to the work of Stroppa and Yvon (2005) and Damper and Eastmond (1997) on sequence-global analogy-based models for morpho-phonological processing, since the main difference between this related work and ours is that both alternatives are based on working units of variable width, rather than our fixed-width n-grams, and also their analogical reasoning is based on interestingly different principles than our k-nearest neighbor classification rule, such as the use of analogical proportions by Stroppa and Yvon (2005).

Acknowledgements

This research was funded by NWO, the Netherlands Organization for Scientific Research, as part of the *IMIX* Programme. The authors would like to thank Walter Daelemans for fruitful discussions, and three anonymous reviewers for their insightful comments.

References

D. W. Aha, D. Kibler, and M. Albert. 1991. Instance-based learning algorithms. *Machine Learning*, 6:37–66.

R. H. Baayen, R. Piepenbrock, and H. van Rijn. 1993. *The CELEX lexical data base on CD-ROM*. Linguistic Data Consortium, Philadelphia, PA.

W. Daelemans, J. Zavrel, K. Van der Sloot, and A. Van den Bosch. 2004. TiMBL: Tilburg memory based learner, version 5.1.0, reference guide. Technical Report ILK 04-02, ILK Research Group, Tilburg University.

R. I. Damper and J. F. G. Eastmond. 1997. Pronunciation by analogy: impact of implementational choices on performance. *Language and Speech*, 40:1–23.

E. Daya, D. Roth, and S. Wintner. 2004. Learning Hebrew roots: Machine learning with linguistic constraints. In Dekang Lin and Dekai Wu, editors, *Proceedings of EMNLP 2004*, pages 357–364, Barcelona, Spain, July. Association for Computational Linguistics.

A.P. Dempster, N.M. Laird, and D.B. Rubin. 1977. Maximum likelihood from incomplete data via the EM algorithm. *Journal of the Royal Statistical Society, Series B (Methodological)*, 39(1):1–38.

T. G. Dietterich, H. Hild, and G. Bakiri. 1995. A comparison of ID3 and backpropagation for English text-to-speech mapping. *Machine Learning*, 19(1):5–28.

E. Noreen. 1989. *Computer-intensive methods for testing hypotheses: an introduction*. John Wiley and sons.

A. Prince and P. Smolensky. 2004. *Optimality Theory: Constraint Interaction in Generative Grammar*. Blackwell Publishers.

V. Punyakanok and D. Roth. 2001. The use of classifiers in sequential inference. In *NIPS-13; The 2000 Conference on Advances in Neural Information Processing Systems*, pages 995–1001. The MIT Press.

T.J. Sejnowski and C.S. Rosenberg. 1987. Parallel networks that learn to pronounce english text. *Complex Systems*, 1:145–168.

N. Stroppa and F. Yvon. 2005. An analogical learner for morphological analysis. In *Proceedings of the 9th Conference on Computational Natural Language Learning*, pages 120–127. Association for Computational Linguistics.

K. Torkkola. 1993. An efficient way to learn English grapheme-to-phoneme rules automatically. In *Proceedings of the International Conference on Acoustics, Speech, and Signal Processing (ICASSP)*, volume 2, pages 199–202, Minneapolis.

A. Van den Bosch and W. Daelemans. 1993. Data-oriented methods for grapheme-to-phoneme conversion. In *Proceedings of the 6th Conference of the EACL*, pages 45–53.

A. Van den Bosch and W. Daelemans. 1999. Memory-based morphological analysis. In *Proceedings of the 37th Annual Meeting of the ACL*, pages 285–292, San Francisco, CA. Morgan Kaufmann.

A. Van den Bosch and W. Daelemans. 2005. Improving sequence segmentation learning by predicting trigrams. In I. Dagan and D. Gildea, editors, *Proceedings of the Ninth Conference on Computational Natural Language Learning*.

A. Weijters. 1991. A simple look-up procedure superior to NETtalk? In *Proceedings of the International Conference on Artificial Neural Networks - ICANN-91, Espoo, Finland*.

F. Yvon. 1996. *Prononcer par analogie: motivation, formalisation et évaluation*. Ph.D. thesis, Ecole Nationale Supérieure des Télécommunication, Paris.

Richness of the Base and Probabilistic Unsupervised Learning in Optimality Theory

Gaja Jarosz
Department of Cognitive Science
Johns Hopkins University
Baltimore, MD 21218
jarosz@cogsci.jhu.edu

Abstract

This paper proposes an unsupervised learning algorithm for Optimality Theoretic grammars, which learns a complete constraint ranking and a lexicon given only unstructured surface forms and morphological relations. The learning algorithm, which is based on the Expectation-Maximization algorithm, gradually maximizes the likelihood of the observed forms by adjusting the parameters of a probabilistic constraint grammar and a probabilistic lexicon. The paper presents the algorithm's results on three constructed language systems with different types of hidden structure: voicing neutralization, stress, and abstract vowels. In all cases the algorithm learns the correct constraint ranking and lexicon. The paper argues that the algorithm's ability to identify correct, restrictive grammars is due in part to its explicit reliance on the Optimality Theoretic notion of Richness of the Base.

1 Introduction

In Optimality Theory or OT (Prince and Smolensky, 1993) grammars are defined by a set of ranked universal and violable constraints. The function of the grammar is to map underlying or lexical forms to valid surface forms. The task of the learner is to find the correct grammar, or correct ranking of constraints, as well as the set of underlying forms that correspond to overt surface forms given only the surface forms and the set of universal constraints.

The most well known algorithms for learning OT grammars (Tesar, 1995; Tesar and Smolensky, 1995; Boersma, 1997, 1998; Prince and Tesar, 1999; Boersma and Hayes, 2001) are supervised learners and focus on the task of learning the constraint ranking, given training pairs that map underlying forms to surface forms. Recent work has focused on the task of unsupervised learning of OT grammars, where only unstructured surface forms are provided to the learner. Some of this work focuses on grammar learning without training data (Tesar, 1998; Tesar, 1999; Hayes, 2004; Apoussidou and Boersma, 2004). The remainder of this work tackles the problem of learning the ranking and lexicon simultaneously, the problem addressed in the present paper (Tesar et al., 2003; Tesar, 2004; Tesar and Prince, to appear; Merchant and Tesar, to appear). These proposals adopt an algebraic approach wherein learning the lexicon involves iteratively eliminating potential underlying forms by determining that they have become logically impossible, given certain assumptions about the learning problem.[1] In particular, one simplifying assumption of previous work requires that mappings be one-to-one and onto. This assumption prohibits input-output mappings with deletion and insertion as well as

[1] An alternative algorithm is proposed in Escudero (2005), but it has not been tested computationally.

Proceedings of the Eighth Meeting of the ACL Special Interest Group on Computational Phonology at HLT-NAACL 2006, pages 50–59,
New York City, USA, June 2006.

constraints that evaluate such mappings. This work represents a leap forward toward the accurate modeling of human language acquisition, but the identification of a general-purpose, unsupervised learner of OT remains an open problem.

In contrast to previous work, this paper proposes a gradual, probabilistic algorithm for unsupervised OT learning based on the Expectation Maximization algorithm (Dempster et al., 1977). Because the algorithm depends on gradually maximizing an objective function, rather than on wholly eliminating logically impossible hypotheses, it is not crucial to prohibit insertion or deletion.

A major challenge posed by unsupervised learning of OT is that of learning *restrictive* grammars that generate only grammatical forms. In previous work, the preference for restrictive grammars is implemented by encoding a bias into the ranking algorithm that favors ranking constraints that prohibit marked structures as high as possible. In contrast, the solution proposed here involves a combination of likelihood maximization and explicit reliance on *Richness of the Base,* an OT principle requiring that the set of potential underlying forms be universal. This combination favors restrictive grammars because grammars that map a "rich" lexicon onto observed forms with high probability are preferred. The proposed model is tested on three constructed language systems, each exemplifying a different type of hidden structure.

2 Learning Probabilistic OT

While the primary task of the grammar is to map underlying forms to overt forms, the grammar's secondary role is that of a filter – ruling out ungrammatical forms no matter what underlying form is fed to the grammar. The role of the grammar as filter follows from the OT principle of Richness of the Base, according to which the set of possible underlying forms is universal (Prince and Smolensky 1993). In other words, the grammar must be restrictive and not over-generate. The requirement that grammars be restrictive complicates the learning problem - it is not sufficient to find a combination of underlying forms and constraint ranking that yields the set of observed surface forms: the constraint ranking must yield only grammatical forms irrespective of the particular lexical items selected for the language.

In classic OT, constraint ranking is categorical and non-probabilistic. In recent years various stochastic versions of OT have been proposed to account for free variation (Boersma and Hayes, 2001), lexically conditioned variation (Anttila, 1997), child language acquisition (Legendre et al., 2002) and the modeling of frequencies associated with these phenomena. In addition to these advantages, probabilistic versions of OT are advantageous from the point of view of learnability. In particular, the Gradual Learning Algorithm for Stochastic OT (Boersma, 1997, 1998; Boersma and Hayes, 2001) is capable of learning in spite of noisy training data and is capable of learning variable grammars in a supervised fashion. In addition, probabilistic versions of OT and variants of OT (Goldwater and Johnson, 2003; Rosenbach and Jaeger, 2003) enable learning of OT via likelihood maximization, for which there exist many established algorithms. Furthermore, as this paper proposes, unsupervised learning of OT using likelihood maximization combined with Richness of the Base provides a natural solution to the grammar-as-filter problem due to the power of probabilistic modeling to use negative evidence implicitly.

The algorithm proposed here relies on a probabilistic extension of OT in which each possible constraint ranking is assigned a probability P(r). Thus, the OT grammar is a probability distribution over constraint rankings rather than a single constraint ranking. This notion of probabilistic OT is similar to - but less restricted than - Stochastic OT, in which the distribution over possible rankings is given by the joint probability over independently normally distributed constraints with fixed, equal variance. The advantage of the present model is computational simplicity, but the proposed learning algorithm does not depend on any particular instantiation of probabilistic OT.

Tables 1 and 2 illustrate the proposed probabilistic version of OT with an abstract example. Table 1 shows the violation marks assigned by three constraints, A, B and C, to five candidate outputs O_1-O_5 for the underlying form, or input /I/. To compute the winner of an optimization, constraints are applied to the candidate set in order according to their rank. Candidates continue to the next constraint if they have the fewest (or tie for fewest) constraint violation marks (indicated by asterisks). In this way the winning or optimal candidate, the candidate that violates the higher-ranked constraints the least, is selected.

		constraints		
input:	/I/	A	B	C
candidates	O_1	*	*	
	O_2	**		*
	O_3		**	
	O_4		*	**
	O_5	*		**

Table 1. OT Candidates and Constraint Violations

The third column of Table 2 identifies the winner under each possible ranking of the three constraints. For example, if the ranking is A >> B >> C, constraint A eliminates all but O_3 and O_4, then constraint B eliminates O_3, designating O_4 as the winner. The remainder of Table 2 illustrates the proposed probabilistic instantiation of OT. The first column shows the probability P(r) that the grammar assigns to each ranking in this example. The probability of each ranking determines the probability with which the winner under that ranking will be selected for the given input. In other words, it defines the conditional probability $P_r(O_k \mid I)$, shown in the fourth column, of the kth output candidate given the input /I/ under the ranking r. The last column shows the total conditional probability for each candidate after summing across rankings. For instance, O_3 is the winner under two of the rankings, and thus its total conditional probability $P(O_3 \mid I)$ is found by summing over the conditional probabilities under each ranking. The total conditional probability $P(O_3 \mid I)$ refers to the probability that underlying form /I/ will surface as O_3, and this probability depends on the grammar.

P(r)	ranking	winner	***$P_r(O_k \mid I)$***	***$P(O_k \mid I)$***
0.20	A>>B>>C	O_4	0.2	0.2
0.15	A>>C>>B	O_3	0.15	0.2
0.05	C>>A>>B	O_3	0.05	
0.10	B>>A>>C	O_5	0.1	0.1
0.00	B>>C>>A	O_2	0.0	0.0
0.50	C>>B>>A	O_1	0.5	0.5

Table 2: Probabilistic OT

In addition to the conditional probability assigned by the grammar, this model relies on a probability distribution $P(I \mid M)$ over possible underlying forms for a given morpheme M. This property of the model implements the standard linguistic proposition that each morpheme has a consistent underlying form across contexts, while the grammar drives allomorphic variation that may result in the morpheme having different surface realizations in different contexts. Rather than identifying a single underlying form for each morpheme, this model represents the underlying form as a distribution over possible underlying forms, and this distribution is constant across contexts. To determine the probability of an underlying form for a morphologically complex word, the product of the morpheme's individual distributions is taken – the probability of an underlying form is taken to be independent of morphological context. For example, suppose that some morpheme M_k has two possible underlying forms, I_1 and I_2, and the two underlying forms are equally likely. This means that the conditional probabilities of both underlying forms are 50%: $P(I_1 \mid M_k) = P(I_2 \mid M_k) = 50\%$.

In sum, the probabilistic model described here consists of a grammar and lexicon, both of which are probabilistic. The task of learning involves selecting the appropriate parameter settings of both the grammar and lexicon simultaneously.

3 Expectation Maximization and Richness of the Base in OT

This section presents the details of the learning algorithm for probabilistic OT. First, in Section 3.1 the objective function and its properties are discussed. Next, Section 3.2 proposes the solution to the grammar-as-filter problem, which involves restricting the search space available to the learning algorithm. Finally, Section 3.3 describes the likelihood maximization algorithm – the input to the algorithm, the initial state, and the form of the solution.

3.1 The Objective Function

The learning algorithm relies on the following objective function:

$$P_H(O \mid M) = \prod_k [P_H(O_k \mid M_k)]^{F_k}$$
$$= \prod_k [\sum_j P_H(O_k \,\&\, I_{k,j} \mid M_k)]^{F_k}$$
$$= \prod_k [\sum_j P_H(O_k \mid I_{k,j}) P_H(I_{k,j} \mid M_k)]^{F_k}$$

The likelihood of the data, or set of overt surface forms, $P_H(O \mid M)$ depends on the parameter settings, the probability distributions over rankings and underlying forms, under the hypothesis H. It is also conditional on M, the set of observed morphemes, which are annotated in the data provided to the algorithm. M is constant, however, and does not differ between hypotheses for the same data set. Under this model each unique surface form O_k is treated independently, and the likelihood of the data is simply the product of the probability of each surface form, raised to the power corresponding to its observed frequency F_k. Each surface form O_k is composed of a set of morphemes M_k, and each of these morphemes has a set of underlying forms $I_{k,j}$. The probability of each surface form $P_H(O_k \mid M_k)$ is found by summing the joint distribution $P_H(O_k \& I_{k,j} \mid M_k)$ over all possible underlying forms $I_{k,J}$ for morphemes M_k that compose O_k. Finally, the joint probability is simply the product of the conditional probability $P_H(O_k \mid I_{k,j})$ and lexical probability $P_H(I_{K,j} \mid M_k)$, both of which were defined in the previous section.

The primary property of this objective function is that it is maximal only when the hypothesis generates the observed data with high probability. In other words, the grammar must map the selected lexicon onto observed surface forms without wasting probability mass on unobserved forms. Because there are two parameters in the model, this can be accomplished by adjusting the ranking distributions or by adjusting lexicon distributions. The probability model itself does not specify whether the grammar or the lexicon should be adjusted in order to maximize the objective function. In other words, the objective function is indifferent to whether the restrictions observed in the language are accounted for by having a restrictive grammar or by selecting a restrictive lexicon. As discussed in Section 2, according to Richness of the Base, only the first option is available in OT: the grammar must be restrictive and must neutralize noncontrastive distinctions in the language. The next subsection addresses the proposed solution – a restriction of the search procedure that favors maximizing probability by restricting the grammar rather than the lexicon.

3.2 Richness of the Base

Although the notion of a restrictive grammar is intuitively clear, it is difficult to implement formally. Previous work on OT learnability (Tesar, 1995; Tesar and Smolensky, 1995; Smolensky 1996; Tesar, 1998, Tesar, 1999; Tesar et al., 2003; Tesar and Prince, to appear; Hayes, 2004) has proposed the heuristic of *Markedness over Faithfulness* during learning to favor restrictive grammars. In OT there are two basic types of constraints, markedness constraints, which penalize dispreferred surface structures, and faithfulness constraints, which penalize nonidentical mappings from underlying to surface forms. In general, a restrictive grammar will have markedness constraints ranked high, because these constraints will restrict the type of surface forms that are allowed in a language. On the other hand, if faithfulness constraints are ranked high, all the distinctions introduced into the lexicon will surface. Thus, a heuristic preferring markedness constraints to rank high whenever possible does in general prefer restrictive grammars. However, the markedness over faithfulness heuristic does not exhaust the notion of restrictiveness. In particular, markedness over faithfulness does not favor grammar restrictiveness that follows from particular rankings between markedness constraints or between faithfulness constraints.

This work aims to provide a general solution that does not require distinguishing various types of constraints – the proposed solution implements Richness of the Base explicitly in the initial state of the lexicon. Specifically, the solution involves requiring that initial distributions over the lexicon be uniform, or rich. Although the objective function alone does not prefer restrictive grammars over restrictive lexicons, a lexicon constrained to be uniform, or nonrestrictive, will in turn force the grammar to be restrictive. Another way to think about it is that a restrictive grammar is one that compresses the input distributions maximally by mapping as much of the lexicon onto observed surface forms as possible. By requiring the lexicon to be rich the proposed solution relies on the objective function's natural preference for grammars that maximally compress the lexicon. The objective function prefers restrictive grammars in this situation because restrictive grammars will allow the highest probability to be assigned to observed forms. In contrast, if the lexicon is not rich, there is nothing for the grammar to compress, and the objective function's natural preference for compression will not be employed. The next subsection discusses the algorithm and the initialization of the parameters in more detail.

3.3 Likelihood Maximization Algorithm

As discussed above, the goal of the learning algorithm is to find the probability distributions over rankings and lexicons that maximize the probability assigned to the observed set of data according to the objective function. In addition, any regularities present in the data should be accommodated by the grammar rather than by restricting the lexicon. As in previous work on unsupervised learning of OT, the algorithm assumes knowledge of OT constraints, the possible underlying forms of overt forms, and sets of candidate outputs and their constraint violation profiles for all possible underlying forms. While the present version of the algorithm receives this information as input, recent work in computational OT (Riggle, 2004; Eisner, 2000) suggests that this information is formally derivable from the constraints and overt surface forms and can be generated automatically.

In addition, the algorithm receives information about the morphological relations between observed surface forms. Specifically, output forms are segmented into morphemes, and the morphemes are indexed by a unique identifier. This information, which has also been assumed in previous work, cannot be derived directly from the constraints and observed forms but is a necessary component of a model that refers to underlying forms of morphemes. The present work assumes this information is available to the learner although Section 5 will discuss the possibility of learning these morphological relations in conjunction with the learning of phonology.

The set of potential underlying forms is derived from observed surface forms, morphological relations, and the constraint set. On the one hand the set of potential underlying forms, which is initially uniformly distributed, should be rich enough to constitute a rich base for the reasons discussed earlier. On the other hand, the set should be restricted enough so that the search space is not too large and so that the grammar is not pressured to favor mapping underlying forms to completely unrelated surface forms. For this reason, potential underlying forms are derived from surface forms by considering all featural variants of surface forms for features that are evaluated by the grammar. Of these potential underlying forms, only those that can yield each of the observed surface allomorphs of the morpheme under some ranking of the constraints are included. This formulation differs substantially from previous work, which aimed to construct the lexicon via discrete steps, the first of which involved permanently setting the values for features that do not alternate. In contrast, the approach taken here aims to create a rich initial lexicon, to compel the selection of a restrictive grammar.

In addition to featural variants, variants of surface forms that differ in length are included if they are supported by allomorphic alternation. In particular, featural variants of all the observed surface allomorphs of the morpheme are considered as potential underlying forms for the morpheme if each of the observed surface forms can be generated under some ranking. Including these types of underlying forms extends previous work, which did not allow segmental insertion or deletion or constraints that evaluate these unfaithful mappings, such as MAX and DEP.

The algorithm initializes both the lexicon and grammar to uniform probability distributions. This means that all rankings are initially equally likely. Likewise, all potential underlying forms for a morpheme are initially equally likely. Thus, the probability distributions begin unbiased, but choosing an unbiased lexicon initially begins the search through parameter space at a position that favors restrictive grammars. The experiments in the following section suggest that this choice of initialization correctly selects a restrictive final grammar.

The learning algorithm itself is based on the Expectation Maximization algorithm (Dempster et al., 1977) and alternates between an expectation stage and a maximization stage. During the expectation stage the algorithm computes the likelihood of the observed surface forms under the current hypothesis. During the maximization stage the algorithm adjusts the grammar and lexicon distributions in order to increase the likelihood of the data. The probability distribution over rankings is adjusted according to the following re-estimation formula:

$$P_{H+1}(r) = \sum_k \frac{F_k}{\sum_k F_k} \cdot \frac{P_H(O_k \mid r, M_k)}{P_H(O_k \mid M_k)}$$

Intuitively, this formula re-estimates the probability of a ranking for state *H+1* in proportion to the ranking's contribution to the overall probability at state *H*. The algorithm re-estimates the probability distribution for an underlying form according to an analogous formula:

$$P_{H+1}(I_{k,j} \mid M_i) = \sum_k \frac{F_k}{\sum_k F_k} \cdot \frac{P_H(O_k \,\&\, I_{k,j} \mid M_i)}{P_H(O_k \mid M_i)}$$

Intuitively, the re-estimate of the probability of an underlying form $I_{k,j}$ for state *H+1* is proportional to the contribution that underlying form makes to the total probability due to morpheme M_i at state *H*. The algorithm continues to alternate between the two stages until the distributions converge, or until the change between one stage and the next reaches some predetermined minimum. At this point the resulting distributions are taken to correspond to the learned grammar and lexicon.

4 Experiments

This section describes the results of experiments with three artificial language systems with different types of hidden structure. In all experiments presented here, each unique surface form is assumed to occur with frequency 1.

4.1 Voicing Neutralization

The first test set is an artificial language system (Tesar and Prince, to appear) exhibiting voicing neutralization. The constraint set includes five constraints:

- NoVoi - No voiced obstruents
- NoSFV- No syllable-final voiced obstruents
- IVV - No intervocalic voiceless consonants
- IDVoi - Surface voicing must match underlying voicing
- Max - Input segments must have output correspondents

These five constraints can describe a number of languages, but of particular interest are languages in which voicing contrasts are neutralized in one or more positions. Such languages, three of which are shown below, test the algorithm's ability to identify correct and restrictive grammars. The partial rankings shown below correspond to the necessary rankings that must hold for these languages; each partial ranking actually corresponds to several total rankings of the constraints. Also shown below are the morphologically analyzed surface forms for each language that are provided as input to the algorithm. The subscripts in these forms indicate morpheme identities, while the hyphens segment the words into separate morphemes. For example, $\text{tat}_{1,2}$ means that the surface form "tat" could be derived from either morpheme 1 or 2 in this language.

- (A) Final devoicing, contrast intervocalically:
  - NoSFV, Max >> IDVoi >> IVV, NoVoi
  - $\text{tat}_{1,2}$; $\text{dat}_{3,4}$; $\text{tat}_1\text{-e}_5$; $\text{tad}_2\text{-e}_5$; $\text{dat}_3\text{-e}_5$; $\text{dad}_4\text{-e}_5$
- (B) Final devoicing and intervocalic voicing:
  - NoSFV, Max, IVV >> IDVoi, NoVoi
  - $\text{tat}_{1,2}$; $\text{dat}_{3,4}$; $\text{tad}_{1,2}\text{-e}_5$; $\text{dad}_{3,4}\text{-e}_5$
- (C) No voiced obstruents:
  - Max, NoVoi >> IDVoi, IVV
  - $\text{tat}_{1,2,3,4}$; $\text{tat}_{1,2,3,4}\text{-e}_5$

In language C, it would be possible to maximize the objective function by selecting a restrictive lexicon rather than a restrictive grammar. In particular, /tat/ could be selected as the underlying form for morphemes 1-4 in order to account for the lack of voiced obstruents in the observed surface forms. In this case, the objective function could just as well be satisfied by an identity grammar mapping underlying /tat/ to surface "tat". However, as discussed in Section 2, such a grammar would violate the principle of Richness of the Base by putting the restriction against voiced obstruents into the lexicon rather than the grammar. Thus, this language tests not only whether the algorithm finds a maximum, but also whether the maximum corresponds to a restrictive grammar.

In fact, for all three languages above, the algorithm converges on the correct, restrictive grammars and correct lexicons. Specifically, the final grammars for each of the languages above converge on probability distributions that distribute the probability mass equally among the total rankings consistent with the partial orders above. For example, for language C the algorithm converges on a distribution that assigns equal probability to the 20 total rankings consistent with the partial order given by MAX, NOVOI >> IDVOI, IVV.

The initial uniform lexicon for language C is shown in Table 3. Here the numbers 1-5 refer to morpheme indices, and the possible underlying forms for each morpheme are uniformly distributed. This initial lexicon favors a grammar that can map as much of the rich lexicon as possible onto surface forms with no voiced obstruents. With these constraints, this translates into ranking NOVOI above IDVOI and IVV. As the algorithm begins learning the lexicon and continues to refine its hypothesis for this language, nothing drives the algorithm to abandon the initial rich lexicon. Thus, in the final state, the lexicon for this language is identical to the initial lexicon. In general, the final lexicon will be uniformly distributed over underlying forms that differ in noncontrastive features.

1	/tat/ - 25%	/tad/ - 25%	/dat/ - 25%	/dad/ - 25%
2	/tat/ - 25%	/tad/ - 25%	/dat/ - 25%	/dad/ - 25%
3	/tat/ - 25%	/tad/ - 25%	/dat/ - 25%	/dad/ - 25%
4	/tat/ - 25%	/tad/ - 25%	/dat/ - 25%	/dad/ - 25%
5	/e/ - 100%			

Table 3. Initial Lexicon for Language C

4.2 Grammatical and Lexical Stress

The next set of languages from the PAKA system (Tesar et al., 2003) test the ability of the algorithm to identify grammatical stress (most restrictive), lexical stress (least restrictive), and combinations of the two. The constraint set includes:

- MAINLEFT - Stress the leftmost syllable
- MAINRIGHT - Stress the rightmost syllable
- FAITHACCENT - Stress an accented syllable
- FAITHACCENTROOT - Stress an accented root syllable

Possible languages and their corresponding partial orders ranging from least restrictive to most restrictive are shown below. In the first two languages, the least restrictive languages, lexical distinctions in stress are realized faithfully, while grammatical stress surfaces only in forms with no underlying stress. In the final two languages stress is entirely grammatical; underlying distinctions are neutralized in favor of a regular surface stress pattern. Finally, the middle language is a combination of lexical and grammatical stress, requiring that the algorithm learn that a contrast in roots is preserved, while a contrast in suffixes is neutralized.

- Full contrast: roots and suffixes contrast in stress, default left:
  - F >> ML >> MR, FAR
  - pá$_1$-ka$_3$; pa$_1$-gá$_4$; bá$_2$-ka$_3$; bá$_2$-ga$_4$
- Full contrast: roots and suffixes contrast in stress, default right:
  - F >> MR >> ML, FAR
  - pa$_1$-ká$_3$; pa$_1$-gá$_4$; bá$_2$-ka$_3$; ba$_2$-gá$_4$
- Root contrast only, default right:
  - FAR >> MR >> ML
  - pa$_1$-ká$_3$; pa$_1$-gá$_4$; bá$_2$-ka$_3$; bá$_2$-ga$_4$
- Predictable left stress:
  - ML >> FAR, F, MR
  - pá$_1$-ka$_3$; pá$_1$-ga$_4$; bá$_2$-ka$_3$; bá$_2$-ga$_4$
- Predictable right stress:
  - MR >> FAR, F, ML
  - pa$_1$-ká$_3$; pa$_1$-gá$_4$; ba$_2$-ká$_3$; ba$_2$-gá$_4$

In all cases the algorithm learns the correct, restrictive grammars corresponding to the partial orders shown above. As before, the final lexicon assigns uniform probability to all underlying forms that differ in noncontrastive features. For example, in the case of the language with root contrast only, the final lexicon selects a unique lexical item for root morphemes and maintains a uniform probability distribution over stressed and unstressed underlying forms for suffixes.

4.3 Abstract Underlying Vowels

The final experiment tests the algorithm on an artificial language, based on Polish, with abstract underlying vowels that never surface faithfully. Although the particular phenomenon exhibited by Slavic alternating vowels is rare, the general phenomenon wherein underlying forms do not correspond to any surface allomorph is not uncommon and should be accommodated by the learning algorithm. This language presents a challenge for previous work on unsupervised learning of OT because alternations in the number of segments are observed in morpheme 3. The morphologically annotated input to the algorithm for this language is shown in Table 4.

$kater_1$	$vatr_2$	$sater_3$
$kater_1$-a_4	$vatr_2$-a_4	$satr_3$-a_4

Table 4. Yer Language Surface Forms

In this language morphemes 1, 2 and 4 exhibit no alternation while morpheme 3 alternates between *sater* and *satr* depending on the context. The constraints for this language, based on Jarosz (2005), are shown below:

- *E = *[+HIGH][-ATR]
- DEP-V
- MAX-V
- *COMPLEXCODA
- IDENT[HIGH]

1	2	3	4
/kater/	/vatr/	/satEr/	/-a/

Table 5. Desired Final Lexicon

In the proposed analysis of this language, the abstract underlying [E], which is a [+high] version of [e], is neutralized on the surface and exhibits two repairs systematically depending on the context. It deletes in general, but if a complex coda is at stake, the vowel surfaces as [e] by violating IDENT[HIGH]. The required partial ranking for this language is shown below while the desired lexicon is shown in Table 5.

{*E, {DEP-V >> *COMPLEXCODA }} >> IDENT[HIGH] >> MAX-V

The algorithm successfully learns the correct ranking above and the lexicon in Table 5. Specifically, the final grammar assigns equal probability to all the rankings consistent with the above partial order. The final lexicon selects a single underlying form for each morpheme as shown in Table 5 because all underlying distinctions in this language are contrastive.

4.4 Discussion

In summary, the algorithm is able to find a correct grammar and lexicon combination for all of the language systems discussed. As discussed in Section 3, the objective function itself does not favor restrictive grammars, but the ability of the algorithm to learn restrictive grammars in these experiments suggests that initializing the lexicons to uniform distributions does compel the learning algorithm to select restrictive grammars rather than restrictive lexicons.

While the experiments presented in this section focus on the task of learning a grammar and lexicon simultaneously, the proposed algorithm is also capable of learning grammars from structurally ambiguous forms. The same likelihood maximization procedure proposed here could be used for unsupervised learning of grammars that assign full structural description to overt forms. Future directions include testing the algorithm on language data of this sort.

5 Conclusion

In sum, this paper has presented an unsupervised, probabilistic algorithm for OT learning. The paper argues that combining the OT principle of Richness of the Base and likelihood maximization provides a novel and general solution to the problem of finding a restrictive grammar. The proposed solution involves explicitly implementing Richness of the Base in the initialization of the lexicon in order to fully utilize the properties of the objective function. By relying on Richness of the Base and likelihood maximization, the algorithm is able to use negative evidence implicitly to find restrictive grammars. The algorithm is shown to be successful on three constructed languages featuring different types of neutralization and hidden structure.

One potential extension of the proposed algorithm involves combining a system for unsupervised learning of morphological relations with the proposed algorithm for learning phonology. Several algorithms have been proposed for automatically inducing morphological relations, like those assumed by the present learner (Goldsmith, 2001; Snover and Brent, 2001). The task of uncovering morphological relations is complicated by allomorphic alternations that obscure the underlying identity of related morphemes. While these algorithms are very promising, their performance may be significantly enhanced if they were combined with an algorithm that models such phonological alternations.

In conclusion, this is the first proposed unsupervised algorithm for OT learning that takes advantage of the power of probabilistic modeling to learn a grammar and lexicon simultaneously. This paper demonstrates that combining OT theoretic principles with results from computational language learning is a worthwhile pursuit that may inform both disciplines. In this case the theoretical principle of Richness of the Base has provided a novel solution to a learning problem, but at the same time, this work also informs theoretical OT by providing a formal characterization of this theoretical principle. Future work includes testing on larger, more realistic languages, including language data with noise and variation, in order to determine the algorithm's resistance to noise and ability to model variable grammars like those observed in natural languages and in human language acquisition.

Acknowledgements

I would like to thank Paul Smolensky for his invaluable feedback on this work and for his suggestions on the preparation of this paper. I am also grateful to Luigi Burzio, Robert Frank, Jason Eisner, and members of the Johns Hopkins Linguistics Research Group (especially Joan Chen-Main, Adam Wayment, and Sara Finley) for additional comments and helpful discussion.

References

Apoussidou, Diana and Paul Boersma. 2004. Comparing Different Optimality-Theoretic Learning Algorithms:the Case of Metrical Phonology. *Proceedings of the 2004 Spring Symposium Series of the American Association for Artificial Intelligence.*

Anttila, Arto. 1997. Deriving variation from grammar. In F. Hinskens, R. Van Hout and W. L. Wetzels (eds.) Variation, Change and Phonological Theory. Amsterdam, John Benjamins.

Boersma, Paul. 1997. How we Learn Variation, Optionality, and Probability. *Proc. Institute of Phonetic Sciences of the University of Amsterdam* 21:43-58.

Boersma, P. 1998. *Functional Phonology*. Doctoral Dissertation, University of Amsterdam. The Hague: Holland Academic Graphics.

Boersma, P. and B. Hayes. 2001. Empirical Tests of the Gradual Learning Algorithm. *Linguistic Inquiry* 32(1):45-86.

Dempster, A.P., N.M. Laird, and D.B. Rubin. 1977. Maximum Likelihood from incomplete data via the EM Algorithm. *Journal of Royal Statistics Society.* 39(B):1-38

Eisner, Jason. 2000. Easy and hard constraint ranking in optimality theory: Algorithms and complexity. In Jason Eisner, Lauri Karttunen and Alain Thériault (eds.), *Finite-State Phonology: Proceedings of the 5th Workshop of the ACL Special Interest Group in Computational Phonology (SIGPHON)*, pages 22-33, Luxembourg, August.

Escudero, Paola. 2005. *Linguistic Perception and Second Language Acquisition.Explaining the attainment of optimal phonological categorization.* Doctoral dissertation, Utrecht University.

Goldsmith, John. 2001. Unsupervised Learning of Morphology of a Natural Language. *Computational Linguistics*, 27: 153-198.

Goldwater, Sharon and Mark Johnson. 2003. Learning OT constraint rankings using a maximum entropy model. In Jennifer Spenader, Anders Eriksson and Osten Dahl (eds.), *Proceedings of the Stockholm Workshop on Variation within Optimality Theory.* Stockholm University, pages 111-120.

Hayes, Bruce. 2004. Phonological acquisition in Optimality Theory: the early stages. Appeared 2004 in Kager, Rene, Pater, Joe, and Zonneveld, Wim, (eds.), *Fixing Priorities: Constraints in Phonological Acquisition.* Cambridge University Press.

Jarosz, Gaja. 2005. Polish Yers and the Finer Structure of Output-Output Correspondence. *31st Annual Meeting of the Berkeley Linguistics Society,* Berkeley, California.

Lari, K. and S.J. Young. 1990. The estimation of stochastic context-free grammars using the inside-outside algorithm. *Computer Speech and Language.* 4:35-56

Legendre, Geraldine, Paul Hagstrom, Anne Vainikka and Marina Todorova. 2002. Partial Constraint Ordering in Child French Syntax. to appear *Language Acquisition* 10(3). 189-227.

Merchant, Nazarré, and Bruce Tesar. to appear. Learning underlying forms by searching restricted lexical subspaces. In *The Proceedings of Chicago Linguistics Society* 41. ROA-811.

Pereira, F. and Y. Schabes. 1992. Inside-Outside reestimation from partially bracketed corpora. In *Proceedings of the ACL 1992*, Newark, Delaware.

Prince, Alan and Paul Smolensky. 1993. *Optimality Theory: Constraint Interaction in Generative Grammar.* Technical Report 2, Center for Cognitive Science, Rutgers University.

Prince, Alan, and Bruce Tesar. 1999. Learning phonotactic distributions. Technical Report RuCCS-TR-54, Rutgers Center for Cognitive Science, Rutgers University.

Riggle, Jason. 2004. Generation, Recognition, and Learning in Finite State Optimality Theory. Ph.D. Dissertation, UCLA, Los Angeles, California.

Rosenbach, Anette and Gerhard Jaeger. 2003. Cumulativity in Variation: testing different versions of Stochastic OT empirically. Presented at the *Seventh Workshop on Optimality Theoretic Syntax*, University of Nijmegen.

Smolensky, Paul. 1996. The initial state and `richness of the base' in Optimality Theory. Technical Report JHU-CogSci-96-4, Department of Cognitive Science, Johns Hopkins University.

Snover, Matthew and Michael R. Brent. 2001 A Bayesian Model for Morpheme and Paradigm Identification. In *Proceedings of the 39th Annual Meeting of the ACL*, pages 482-490. Association for Computational Linguistics.

Tesar, Bruce. 1995. *Computational Optimality Theory*. Ph.D. thesis, University of Colorado at Boulder, June.

Tesar, Bruce. 1998. An iterative strategy for language learning. *Lingua* 104:131-145. ROA-177.

Tesar, Bruce. 1999. Robust interpretive parsing in metrical stress theory. In *The Proceedings of Seventeenth West Coast Conference on Formal Linguistics*, pp. 625-639. ROA-262.

Tesar, Bruce. 2004. Contrast analysis in phonological learning. Manuscript, Linguistics Dept., Rutgers University. ROA-695.

Tesar, Bruce, John Alderete, Graham Horwood, Nazarré Merchant, Koichi Nishitani, and Alan Prince. 2003. "Surgery in language learning". In *The Proceedings of Twenty-Second West Coast Conference on Formal Linguistics*, pp. 477-490. ROA-619.

Tesar, Bruce and Alan Prince. to appear. "Using phonotactics to learn phonological alternations." Revised version will appear in *The Proceedings of CLS 39*, Vol. II: The Panels. ROA-620.

Tesar, Bruce and Paul Smolensky. 1995. "The Learnability of Optimality Theory". In *Proceedings of the Thirteenth West Coast Conference on Formal Linguistics*, 122-137.

Morphology Induction from Limited Noisy Data Using Approximate String Matching

Burcu Karagol-Ayan, David Doermann, and **Amy Weinberg**
Institute for Advanced Computer Studies (UMIACS)
University of Maryland
College Park, MD 20742
{burcu,doermann,weinberg}@umiacs.umd.edu

Abstract

For a language with limited resources, a dictionary may be one of the few available electronic resources. To make effective use of the dictionary for translation, however, users must be able to access it using the root form of morphologically deformed variant found in the text. Stemming and data driven methods, however, are not suitable when data is sparse. We present algorithms for discovering morphemes from limited, noisy data obtained by scanning a hard copy dictionary. Our approach is based on the novel application of the longest common substring and string edit distance metrics. Results show that these algorithms can in fact segment words into roots and affixes from the limited data contained in a dictionary, and extract affixes. This in turn allows non native speakers to perform multilingual tasks for applications where response must be rapid, and their knowledge is limited. In addition, this analysis can feed other NLP tools requiring lexicons.

1 Introduction

In order to develop morphological analyzers for languages that have limited resources (either in terms of experienced linguists, or electronic data), we must move beyond data intensive methods developed for rich resource languages that rely on large amounts of data for statistical methods. New approaches that can deal with limited, and perhaps noisy, data are necessary for these languages.

Printed dictionaries often exist for languages before large amounts of electronic text, and provide a variety of information in a structured format. In this paper, we propose *Morphology Induction from Noisy Data (MIND)*, a natural language morphology induction framework that operates on from information in dictionaries, specifically headwords and examples of usage. We use string searching algorithms to morphologically segment words and identify prefixes, suffixes, circumfixes, and infixes in noisy and limited data. We present our preliminary results on two data sources (Cebuano and Turkish), give a detailed analysis of results, and compare them to a state-of-the-art morphology learner. We employ the automatically induced affixes in a simple word segmentation process, decreasing the error rate of incorrectly segmented words by 35.41%.

The next section discusses prior work on morphology learning. In Section 3 and 4, we describe our approach and MIND framework in detail. Section 6 explains the experiments and presents results. We conclude with future work.

2 Related Work

Much of the previous work on morphology learning has been reported on automatically acquiring affix lists. Inspired by works of Harris (1955), Dejean (1998) attempted to find a list of frequent affixes for several languages. He used successor and predecessor frequencies of letters in a given sequence of letters in identifying possible morpheme bound-

Proceedings of the Eighth Meeting of the ACL Special Interest Group on Computational Phonology at HLT-NAACL 2006, pages 60–68,
New York City, USA, June 2006.

aries. The morpheme boundaries are where the predictability of the next letter in the letter sequence is the lowest.

Several researchers (Brent, 1993; Brent et al., 1995; Goldsmith, 2001) used Minimum Description Length (MDL) for morphology learning. Snover and Brent (2001) proposed a generative probability model to identify stems and suffixes. Schone and Jurafsky (2001) used latent semantic analysis to find affixes. Baroni et al. (2002) produced a ranked list of morphologically related pairs from a corpus using orthographic or semantic similarity with minimum edit distance and mutual information metrics. Creutz and Lagus (2002) proposed two unsupervised methods for word segmentation, one based on maximum description length, and one based on maximum likelihood. In their model, words consisted of lengthy sequences of segments and there is no distinction between stems and affixes. The Whole Word Morphologizer (Neuvel and Fulop, 2002) uses a POS-tagged lexicon as input, induces morphological relationships without attempting to discover or identify morphemes. It is also capable of generating new words beyond the learning sample.

Mystem (Segalovich, 2003) uses a dictionary for unknown word guessing in a morphological analysis algorithm for web search engines. Using a very simple idea of morphological similarity, unknown word morphology is taken from all the closest words in the dictionary, where the closeness is the number of letters on its end.

The WordFrame model (Wicentowski, 2004) uses inflection-root pairs, where unseen inflections are transformed into their corresponding root forms. The model works with imperfect data, and can handle prefixes, suffixes, stem-internal vowel shifts, and point-of-affixation stem changes. The WordFrame model can be used for co-training with low-accuracy unsupervised algorithms.

Monson (2004) concentrated on languages with limited resources. The proposed language-independent framework used a corpus of full word forms. Candidate suffixes are grouped into candidate inflection classes, which are then arranged in a lattice structure.

A recent work (Goldsmith et al., 2005) proposed to use string edit distance algorithm as a bootstrapping heuristic to analyze languages with rich morphologies. String edit distance is used for ranking and quantifying the robustness of morphological generalizations in a set of clean data.

All these methods require clean and most of the time large amounts of data, which may not exist for languages with limited electronic resources. For such languages, the morphology induction is still a problem. The work in this paper is applicable to noisy and limited data. String searching algorithms are used with information found in dictionaries to extract the affixes.

3 Approach

Dictionary entries contain headwords, and the examples of how these words are used in context (i.e. examples of usage). Our algorithm assumes that each example of usage will contain at least one instance of the headword, either in its root form, or as one of its morphological variants. For each headword–example of usage pair, we find the headword occurrence in the example of usage, and extract the affix if the headword is in one of its morphological variants. We should note that we do not require the data to be perfect. It may have noise such as OCR errors, and our approach successfully identifies the affixes in such noisy data.

4 Framework

Our framework has two stages, *exact match* and *approximate match*, and uses three string distance metrics, the *longest common substring* (LCS), *approximate string matching with k differences* (k-DIFF), and *string edit distance* (SED). We differentiate between exact and approximate matches and assign two counts for each identified affix, *exact count* and *approximate count*. We require that each affix should have a positive exact count in order to be in the final affix list. Although approximate match can be used to find exact matches to identify prefixes, suffixes, and circumfixes, it is not possible to differentiate between infixes and OCR errors. For these reasons, we process the two cases separately.

First we briefly describe the three metrics we use and the adaptations we made to find the edit operations in SED, and then we explain how we use these metrics in our framework.

4.1 String Searching Algorithms

Longest Common Substring (LCS) Given two strings $p = p_1...p_n$ and $q = q_1...q_m$, LCS finds the longest contiguous sequence appearing in p and q. The longest common substring is not same as the longest common subsequence because the longest common subsequence need not be contiguous.

There is a dynamic programming solution for LCS[1] that finds the longest common substring for two strings with length n and m in $O(nm)$.

String Edit Distance (SED) Given two strings p and q, SED is the minimum number of edit operations which transforms p to q. The edit operations allowed are insertions, deletions, and substitutions. In our algorithm, we set the cost of each edit operation to 1. A solution based on dynamic programming computes the distance between strings in $O(mn)$, where m and n are the lengths of the strings (Wagner and Fischer, 1974).

Approximate string matching with k differences (k-DIFF) Given two strings p and q, the problem of approximate string matching with k differences is finding all the substrings of q which are at a distance less than or equal to a given value k from p. Insertions, deletions and substitutions are all allowed. A dynamic programming solution to this problem is the same as the classical string edit distance solution with one difference: the values of the first row of the table are initialized to 0 (Sellers, 1980). This initialization means that the cost of insertions of letters of q at the beginning of p is zero. The solutions are all the values of the last row of table which are less or equal to k. Consequently, the minimum value on the last row gives us the distance of the closest occurrence of the pattern.

String Edit Distance with Edit Operations (SED-path) In our framework, we are also interested in tracing back the editing operations performed in achieving the minimum cost alignment. In order to obtain the sequence of edit operations, we can work backwards from the complete distance matrix. For two strings p and q with lengths n and m respectively, the cell $L[n, m]$ of the distance matrix L gives us the SED between p and q. To get to the cell $L[n, m]$, we had to come from one of 1) $L[n-1, m]$ (insertion), 2) $L[n, m-1]$ (deletion), or 3) $L[n-1, m-1]$ (substitution). Which of the three options was chosen can be reconstructed given these costs, edit operation costs, and the characters $p[n], q[m]$ of the strings. By working backwards, we can trace the entire path and thus reconstruct the alignment. However, there are ambiguous cases; the same minimum cost may be obtained by a number of edit operation sequences. We adapted the trace of the path for our purposes as explained below.

Let *path* be the list of editing operations to obtain minimum distance, and *SED-path* be the SED algorithm that also returns a *path*. The length of the *path* is $max(n, m)$, and $path[j]$ contains the edit operation to change $q[j]$ (or $p[j]$ if $n > m$). *Path* can contain four different types of operations: Match (M), substitution (S), insertion (I), and deletion (D). Our goal is finding affixes and in case of ambiguity, we employed the following heuristics for finding the SED operations leading the minimum distance:

Case 1: If one string is longer than the other, choose I for extra characters

Case 2: Until an M is found, choose I in case of ambiguity

Case 3: If an M is found previously, choose M/S in case of ambiguity

Case 4: If there is an M between two I's, switch this with the last I

Case 1 ensures that if one word has more characters than the other, an insertion operation is selected for those characters.

If there is an ambiguity, and an M/S or I operation have the same minimum cost, Case 2 gives priority to the insertion operation until a match case is encountered, while Case 3 gives priority to match/substitution operations if a match case was seen previously.

Below example shows how Case 4 helps us to localize all the insertion operations. For the headword–candidate example word pair *abirids* $\rightarrow$ *makaabiríds*, the *path* changes from (1) to (2) using Case 4, and correct prefix is identified as we explain in the next section.

(1) `I M I I I M M M S M M` $\Rightarrow$ Prefix *m-*
(2) `I I I I M M M M S M M` $\Rightarrow$ Prefix *maka-*

[1] http://www.ics.uci.edu/ dan/class/161/notes/6/Dynamic.html

5 Morphology Induction from Noisy Data (MIND)

The MIND framework consists of two stages. In the exact match stage, MIND framework checks if the headword occurs without any changes or errors (i.e. if headword occurs exactly in the example of usage). If no such occurrence is found an approximate match search is performed in second stage. Below we describe these two stages in detail.

5.1 Exact Match

Given a list of (noisy) headword–example of usage pairs (w, E), the exact match first checks if the headword occurs in E in its root form.[2] If the headword cannot be found in E in its root form, for each e_i in E, the longest common substring, $LCS(w, e_i)$, is computed.[3] Let e_l be the e_i that has the longest common substring (l) with w.[4] If $w = l$, and for some suffix s and some prefix p one of the following conditions is true, the affix is extracted.

1. $e_l = ws$ (suffix) or
2. $e_l = pw$ (prefix) or
3. $e_l = pws$ (circumfix)

The extracted affixes are added to the induced affix list, and their *exact counts* are incremented. In the third case *p–s* is treated together as a circumfix.

For the infixes, there is one further step. If $w = w'l$ and $e_l = e'_l l$, we compute $LCS(w', e'_l)$. If $e'_l = w's$, for some suffix s, s is added as an infix to the induced affix list. (This means $e_l = w'sl$ where $w = w'l$.)

The following sample run illustrates how the exact match part identifies affixes. Given the Cebuano headword–example of usage pair (*abtik*) — (*naabtikan sad ku sa bátá*), the word *naabtikan* is marked as the candidate that has the longest common substring with headword *abtik*. These two words have the following alignment, and we extract the circumfix *na–an*. In the illustration below, straight lines represent matches, and short lines ending in square boxes represent insertions.

```
        a b t i k
    ╻ ╻ | | | | | ╻ ╻
    n a a b t i k a n
```

5.2 Approximate Match

When we cannot find an exact match, there may be an approximate match resulting from an error with OCR or morphophonemic rules[5], and we deal with such cases separately in the second part of the algorithm. For each e_i in E, we compute the difference between headword, and example word, *k-DIFF*(w, e_i). The example word that has the minimum difference from the headword is selected as the most likely candidate (e_{cand}). We then find the sequence of the edit operations performed in achieving the minimum distance alignment to transform e_{cand} to w using SED-path algorithm we described above.[6]

Let $cnt(X)$ be the count of X operation in the computed path. If $cnt(I) = 0$, this case is considered as an approximate root form (with OCR errors). The following conditions are considered as possible errors and no further analysis is done for such cases:

$$\begin{aligned} cnt(M) &= 0 \;\; \| \\ cnt(M) &< max(cnt(S), cnt(D), cnt(I)) \;\; \| \\ cnt(M) &< cnt(S) + cnt(D) + cnt(I) \end{aligned}$$

Otherwise, we use the insertion operations at the beginning and at the end of the path to identify the type of the affix (prefix, suffix, or circumfix) and the length of the suffix (number of insertion operations). The identified affix is added to the affix list, and its *approximate count* is incremented. All the other cases are dismissed as errors. In its current state, the infix affixes are not handled in approximate match case.

The following sample shows how approximate match works with noisy data. In the Cebuano input

[2] Headwords consisting of one character are not checked.

[3] In order to reduce the search space, we do not check the example words that are shorter than the headword. Although there are some languages, such as Russian, in which headwords may be longer than the inflected forms, such cases are not in the scope of this paper.

[4] Note that the length of the longest common substring can be at most the length of the headword, in which case the longest common substring is the headword itself.

[5] At this initial version, MIND does not make any distinctions between noise in the data such as OCR errors, and morphophonemic rules. Making this distinction will be one of our future focuses

[6] Computing k-difference, and the edit path can be done in parallel to reduce the computing time.

pair (*ambihas*) — (*ambshása pagbutang ang duha ka silya arun makakitá ang maglingkud sa luyu*), the first word in the example of usage has an OCR error, *i* is misrecognized as *s*. Moreover, there is a vowel change in the word caused by the affix. An exact match of the headword cannot be found in the example of usage. The k-DIFF algorithm returns *ambshása* as the candidate example of usage word, with a distance 2. Then, the SED-path algorithm returns the path *M M M S M S M I*, and algorithm successfully concludes that *a* is the suffix as shown below in illustration (dotted lines represent substitutions).

```
a m b i h a s
| | | : | : | ↑
a m b s h á s a
```

6 Experiments

6.1 Dictionaries

The BRIDGE system (Ma et al., 2003) processes scanned and OCRed dictionaries to reproduce electronic versions and extract information from dictionary entries. We used the BRIDGE system to process two bilingual dictionaries, a Cebuano-English (CebEng) dictionary (Wolff, 1972) and a Turkish-English (TurEng) dictionary (Avery et al., 1974), and extract a list of headword-example of usage pairs for our experiments. The extracted data is not perfect: it has mistagged information, i.e. it may include some information that is not the headword or example of usage, or some useful information may be missing, and OCR errors may occur. OCR errors can be in different forms: Two words can be merged into one, one word can be split into two, or characters can be misrecognized.

Dictionary Dictionary	# of pages	# of hw-ex pairs	# of words
Cebuano-all	1163	27129	206149
Turkish-all	1000	27487	111334
Cebuano-20	20	562	4134
Turkish-20	20	503	1849

Table 1: Details of Data from Two Dictionaries Used in Experiments

Along with the headword–example of usage pairs from more than 1000 pages, we randomly selected 20 pages for detailed analysis. Table 1 provides details of the data from two dictionaries we use in our experiments.

Both Cebuano and Turkish are morphologically rich. Cebuano allows prefixes, suffixes, circumfixes, infixes, while Turkish is an agglunative language. The two dictionaries have different characteristics. The example of usages in CebEng are complete sentences given in italic font while TurEng has phrases, idioms, or complete sentences as examples of usages indicated in bold font.

6.2 Protocol

We ran our algorithm first on all of the data and then on a randomly selected 20 pages from each dictionary. We manually extracted the affixes from each of the 20 pages. We then evaluated the MIND results with this ground truth. During the evaluation, even if the number of an affix in the ground truth and result are same, if they were extracted from different words, this is counted as an error. We also examined the cause of each error in this data.

We then compare our results from the whole TurEng data with the state-of-the-art Linguistica (Goldsmith, 2001) algorithm. Finally, we used the suffixes extracted by MIND and Linguistica to segment words in a Turkish treebank.

6.3 Analysis

Dict.	Affix	Sample words
	mu-	galing/mugaling hikúhíkú/muhikùhíkù
C	nag-	kisdum/nagkisdum kugkugl/nagkugkug
E	mi-	iktin/miiktin kírus/mikárus
B	i-	kunsuylu/ikunsuylu pazíha/iparíha
U	na-	píl/napíl ulatl/naúlat
A	gi-	buga/gibuga dálit/gidádit
N	gi-an	labuk/gilabukan íkug/giikúgan
O	-un	gihay/gihayun gáyung/gayúngun
	-a	pisar/pisara sirnpul/simpúla
	-ı	ad/adı ilaç/ilaeı
T	-i	heves/hevesi ilim/ilmi
U	-a	saz/saza sonsuz/sonsuza
R	-e	deniz/denize zmim/mime
K	-ına	etraf/etrafına kolay/kolayına
I	-ya	hasta/hastaya orta/ortaya
S	-ü	üst/üstü zyüz/yüzü
H	-ini	bel/belini zevk/zevkini
	-ine	derin/derinine iç/içine

Table 3: Sample Affixes Extracted from Two Dictionaries

Table 2 shows result of MIND runs. The total number of affixes and number of different types of

	Cebuano				Turkish			
	Whole dict.		20 pages		Whole dict.		20 pages	
Total	26106		542		27314		502	
Root form	5727		180		18416		345	
Prefix (diff. type)	10300	(180)	197	(26)	6	(6)	0	(0)
Suffix (diff. type)	1315	(253)	16	(8)	6983	(447)	128	(59)
Infix (diff. type)	25	(11)	0	(0)	1	(1)	0	(0)
Circumfix (diff. type)	717	(221)	18	(11)	9	(9)	0	(0)
App. Root form	1023		14		103		1	
App. Prefix (diff. type)	1697	(116)	23	(9)	8	(8)	1	(1)
App. Suffix (diff. type)	2930	(199)	63	(19)	168	(100)	5	(5)
App. Circumfix (diff. type)	1060	(207)	14	(5)	20	(20)	0	(0)
Couldn't decide	1159		13		765		15	

Table 2: Total Number and Different Types of Affixes Extracted from Two Dictionaries Using MIND

affixes (in parenthesis) are presented for two dictionaries, CebEng and TurEng, and two data sets, the whole dictionary and 20 randomly selected pages. The top part of the table gives the exact match results and the bottom part shows the approximate match results. For Cebuano, approximate match part of the framework finds many more affixes than it does for Turkish. This is due to the different structures in the two dictionaries. We should note that although MIND incorrectly finds a few prefixes, circumfixes, and infixes for Turkish, these all have count one. Table 3 contains some of the most frequent extracted affixes along with their exact and approximate counts, and samples of headword–example of usage word pairs they were extracted from. Each word is segmented into one root and one suffix, therefore when a word takes multiple affixes, they are all treated as a compound affix.

Dictionary	GT cnt.	Res.cnt.	Misses	Additions
Cebuano	311	314	17	14
Turkish	155	142	8	10

Table 4: Detailed Analysis of Affixes from 20 Pages

Table 4 shows the number of affixes in ground truth and MIND results along with number of missed and incorrectly added affixes on 20 of these pages of data. MIND only missed 5% of the affixes in the ground truth in both data sets.

We also examined the causes of each miss and addition. Table 5 presents the causes of errors in the output of MIND with an example for each cause. We should emphasize that a valid affix such as Turkish suffix *-mı* is counted as an error since the suffix *-ını* should be extracted for that particular headword–example of usage pair. An OCR error such as the misrecognition of *a* as *d*, causes both the miss of the prefix *mag-* and incorrect addition of *mdg-* for Cebuano. There are some cases that cannot be correctly identified by the framework. These usually involve dropping the last vowel because of morphophonemic rules. For the Cebuano dictionary, merge and split caused several errors, while Turkish data does not have any such errors. Main reason is the different structure and format of the original dictionaries. In the Cebuano dictionary, an italic font which may result in merge and split is used to indicate example of usages.

For the Cebuano data, five invalid suffixes, three invalid prefixes, and two invalid circumfixes are found, while one valid suffix and one valid circumfix are missed. For the Turkish data, three invalid suffixes, one invalid prefix, and two valid suffixes are found while two valid suffix are missed. When we look at the invalid affixes in the data, most of them (six of the Cebuano, and all of the Turkish ones) have count one, and maximum count in an invalid affix is five. Therefore, if we use a low threshold, we can eliminate many of the invalid affixes.

6.4 Comparison to Linguistica

We compared our system with *Linguistica*, a publicly available unsupervised corpus-based morphology learner (Goldsmith, 2001). Linguistica induces paradigms in a noise-free corpus, while MIND makes use of string searching algorithms and allows one to deal with noise at the cost of correctness. MIND emphasize segmenting a word into its root and affixes. We trained Linguistica using two different data sets from TurEng[7]: 1) Whole headword-

[7]We would like to do the same comparison in Cebuano. For the time being, we could not find a treebank and native speakers

Reason	Cebuano		Turkish	
OCR	8	M→lbi	11	ını→mı or ım
Algorithm	8	(uluy, giuylan)→ not gi-an, -lan is found	7	(alın, alnında)→ not -ında, -da is found
Merge	9	ímung giláug→ímunggiláug	0	-
Split	1	nag-kúgus→nag- kúgus	0	-
Other	5	apr.→april Headword is an abbreviation	0	-

Table 5: The Distribution of the Causes of Errors in 20 Pages with Samples

example of usage sentence pairs, and 2) Headword-candidate example words that our algorithm returns. In the first case (Ling-all), Linguistica uses more data than our algorithm, so to avoid any biases resulting from this, we also trained Linguistica using the headword and candidate example word (Ling-cand). We only used the suffixes, since Turkish is a suffix-based language. The evaluation is done by a native speaker.

Figure 1 presents the analysis of the suffix lists produced by Linguistica using two sets of training data, and MIND. The suffix lists are composed of suffixes the systems return that have counts more than a threshold. The results are presented for six threshold values for all of the data. We use thresholding to decrease the number of invalid affixes caused primarily by the noise in the data. For the MIND results, the suffixes over threshold are the ones that have positive exact counts and total counts (sum of exact and approximate counts) more than the threshold. Although Linguistica is not designed for thresholding, the data we use is noisy, and we explored if suffixes with a corpus count more than a threshold will eliminate invalid suffixes. The table on the left gives the total number of suffixes, the percentage of suffixes that have a count more than a threshold value, the percentage of invalid suffixes, and percentage of missed suffixes that are discarded by thresholding for the whole TurEng dictionary. The number of affixes MIND finds are much more than that of Linguistica. Furthermore, number of invalid affixes are lower. On the other hand, the number of missed affixes is also higher for MIND since, for this particular data, there are many affixes with counts less than 5. 41% of the affixes have an exact count of 1. The main reason for this is the agglunative nature of Turkish language. The effect of thresholding can also be examined in the graph on the right in Figure1 which gives the percentage of valid suffixes as a function of threshold values. MIND takes advantage of thresholding, and percentage of valid suffixes rapidly decrease for threshold value 1.

for Cebuano.

System	Th.	Total	Over Th.	Invalid	Missed
Ling-cand	0	6	100.00	0.00	0.00
Ling-all	0	4	100.00	0.00	0.00
MIND	0	60	96.67	1.72	0.00
Ling-cand	1	6	66.67	0.00	33.33
Ling-all	1	4	100.00	0.00	0.00
MIND	1	60	41.67	0.00	53.33
Ling-cand	2	6	50.00	0.00	50.00
Ling-all	2	4	75.00	0.00	25.00
MIND	2	60	18.33	0.00	76.67

Table 6: Total Number and Percentage of Over the Threshold, Invalid, and Missed Suffixes Found by Linguistica and MIND for Different Threshold Values for 20 pages of Turkish Data

Table 6 presents the same results for 20 pages from TurEng for three threshold values. MIND performs well even with very small data and finds many valid affixes. Linguistica on the other hand finds very few.

6.5 Stemming

To test the utility of the results, we perform a simple word segmentation, with the aim of stripping the inflectional suffixes, and find the bare form of the word. A word segmenter takes a list of suffixes, and their counts from the morphology induction system (Linguistica or MIND), a headword list as a dictionary, a threshold value, and the words from a treebank. For each word in the treebank, there is a root form (rf), and a usage form (uf). The suffixes with a count more than the threshold are indexed according to their last letters. For each word in the treebank, we first check if uf is already in the dictionary, i.e. in the headword list. If we cannot find it

System	Th.	Total	% Over Th.	% Invalid	% Missed
Ling-cand	0	116	100.00	18.10	0.00
Ling-all	0	274	100.00	34.67	0.00
MIND	0	499	89.58	13.20	3.61
Ling-cand	1	116	98.28	17.54	0.86
Ling-all	1	274	94.89	32.69	1.46
MIND	1	499	50.50	4.37	33.07
Ling-cand	2	116	92.24	16.82	5.17
Ling-all	2	274	87.96	31.12	4.74
MIND	2	499	38.48	4.17	44.49
Ling-cand	3	116	91.38	16.98	6.03
Ling-all	3	274	85.40	31.20	6.57
MIND	3	499	28.86	2.78	53.31
Ling-cand	4	116	81.03	12.77	11.21
Ling-all	4	274	81.39	30.94	9.12
MIND	4	499	25.65	3.13	56.51
Ling-cand	5	116	80.17	12.90	12.07
Ling-all	5	274	79.56	31.19	10.58
MIND	5	499	23.25	2.59	58.72

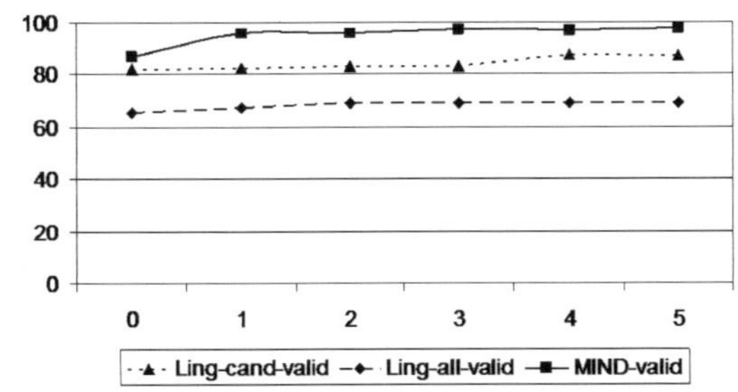

Figure 1: Total Number and Percentage of Over the Threshold, Invalid, Missed and Valid Suffixes Found by Linguistica and MIND for Different Threshold Values

in the dictionary, we repeatedly attempt to find the longest suffix that matches the end of uf, and check the dictionary again. The process stops when a dictionary word is found or when no matching suffixes can be found at the end of the word. If the word the segmenter returns is same as rf in the treebank, we increase the correct count. Otherwise, this case is counted as an error.

In our stemming experiments we used METU-Sabanci Turkish Treebank[8], a morphologically and syntactically annotated treebank corpus of 7262 grammatical sentences (Atalay et al., 2003; Oflazer et al., 2003). We skipped the punctuation and multiple parses,[9] and ran our word segmentation on 14950 unique words. We also used the headword list extracted from TurEng as the dictionary. Note that, the headword list is not error-free, it has OCR errors. Therefore even if the word segmenter returns the correct root form, it may not be in the dictionary and the word may be stripped further.

The percentage of correctly segmented words are presented in Figure 2. We show results for six threshold values. Suffixes with counts more than the threshold are used in each case. Again for MIND results, we require that the exact match counts are more than zero, and the total of exact match and approximate match counts are more than the threshold. For Linguistica, suffixes with a corpus count more than the threshold are used. For each threshold value, MIND did much better than Ling-cand. MIND outperformed Ling-all for thresholds 0 and 1. For the other values, the difference is small. We should note that Ling-all uses much more training data than MIND (503 vs. 1849 example of words), and even with this difference the performance of MIND is close to Ling-all. We believe the reason for the close performance of MIND and Ling-all in segmentation despite the huge difference in the number of correct affixes they found due to the fact that affixes Ling-all finds are shorter, and more frequent. In its current state, MIND does not segment compound affixes, and find several long and less frequent affixes. These long affixes can be composed

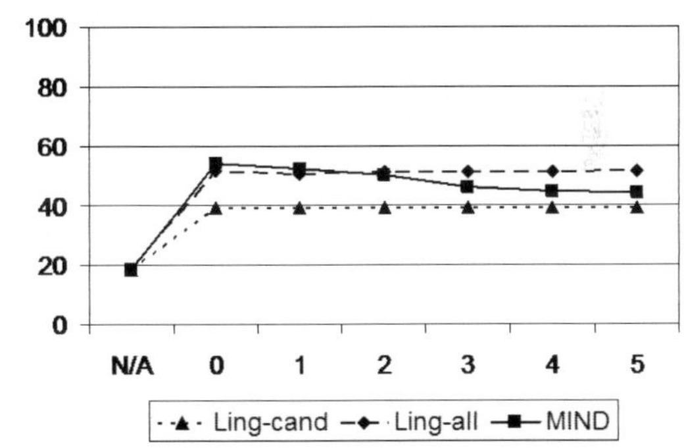

Figure 2: Percentage of Correctly Segmented Words by Different Systems for Different Threshold Values

[8]http://www.ii.metu.edu.tr/ corpus/treebank.html

[9]Multiple parses are the cases where a suffix is attached not to a single word, but to a group of words. The suffix *-ti* in *takip etti* is attached to *takip et*.

by shorter affixes Linguistica finds.

7 Conclusion and Future Work

We presented a framework for morphology induction from noisy data, that is especially useful for languages which have limited electronic data. We use the information in dictionaries, specifically headword and the corresponding example of usage sentences, to acquire affix lists of the language. We presented results on two data sets and demonstrated that our framework successfully finds the prefixes, suffixes, circumfixes, and infixes. We also used the acquired suffix list from one data set in a simple word segmentation process, and outperformed a state-of-the-art morphology learner using the same amount of training data.

At this point we are only using headword and corresponding example of usage pairs. Dictionaries provide much more information. We plan to make use of other information, such as POS, to categorize the acquired affixes. We will also investigate how using all the words in example of usages and splitting the compound affixes in agglunative languages can help us to increase the confidence of correct affixes, and decrease the number of invalid affixes. Finally we will work on identifying morphophonemic rules (especially stem-interval vowel shifts and point-of-affixation stem changes).

Acknowledgments

The partial support of this research under contract MDA-9040-2C-0406 is gratefully acknowledged.

References

Nart B. Atalay, Kemal Oflazer, and Bilge Say. 2003. The annotation process in the Turkish Treebank. In *Proceedings of the EACL Workshop on Linguistically Interpreted Corpora–LINC*, Budapest, Hungary, April.

Robert Avery, Serap Bezmez, Anna G. Edmonds, and Mehlika Yaylalı. 1974. *Redhouse İngilizce-Türkçe Sözlük*. Redhouse Yayınevi.

Marco Baroni, Johannes Matiasek, and Harald Trost. 2002. Unsupervised discovery of morphologically related words based on orthographic and semantic similarity. In *Proceedings of the ACL-02 Workshop on Morphological and Phonological Learning*, pages 48–57.

Michael R. Brent, Sreerama K. Murthy, and Andrew Lundberg. 1995. Discovering morphemic suffixes: A case study in minimum description length induction. In *Proceedings of the 15th Annual Conference of the Cognitive Science Society*, pages 28–36, Hillsdale, NJ.

Michael R. Brent. 1993. Minimal generative models: A middle ground between neurons and triggers. In *Proceedings of the 5th International Workshop on Artificial Intelligence and Statistics*, Ft. Laudersdale, FL.

Mathias Creutz and Krista Lagus. 2002. Unsupervised discovery of morphemes. In *Proceedings of the ACL-02 Workshop on Morphological and Phonological Learning*.

H. Dejean. 1998. Morphemes as necessary concepts for structures: Discovery from untagged corpora. In *Workshop on Paradigms and Grounding in Natural Language Learning*, pages 295–299.

John Goldsmith, Yu Hu, Irina Matveeva, and Colin Sprague. 2005. A heuristic for morpheme discovery based on string edit distance. Technical Report TR-2205-04, Department of Computer Science, University of Chicago.

John Goldsmith. 2001. Unsupervised learning of the morphology of a natural language. *Computational Linguistics*, 27(2):153–198.

Zellig Harris. 1955. From phoneme to morpheme. *Language*, 31:190–222.

Huanfeng Ma, Burcu Karagol-Ayan, David Doermann, Douglas Oard, and Jianqiang Wang. 2003. Parsing and tagging of bilingual dictionaries. *Traitement Automatique Des Langues*, pages 125–150.

Christian Monson. 2004. A framework for unsupervised natural language morphology induction. In *Proceedings of the Student Research Workshop: ACL 2004*, pages 67–72.

Sylvain Neuvel and Sean A. Fulop. 2002. Unsupervised learning of morphology without morphemes. In *Proceedings of the ACL-02 Workshop on Morphological and Phonological Learning*, pages 31–40.

Kemal Oflazer, Bilge Say, Dilek Hakkani-Tür, and Gökhan Tür. 2003. Building a Turkish Treebank. In Anne Abeillé, editor, *Building and Using Parsed Corpora*. Kluwer Academic Publishers.

Patrick Schone and Daniel Jurafsky. 2001. Knowledge-free induction of inflectional morphologies. In *Second Meeting of the NAACL*, pages 183–191.

Ilya Segalovich. 2003. A fast morphological algorithm with unknown word guessing induced by a dictionary for a web search engine. In *Proceedings of MLMTA*, Las Vegas, NV.

P.H. Sellers. 1980. The theory and computation of evolutionary distances: pattern recognition. *Journal of Algorithms*, 1:359–373.

Matthew G. Snover and Michael R. Brent. 2001. A bayesian model for morpheme and paradigm identification. In *Proceedings of the 39th Annual Meeting of the ACL*, pages 482–490.

Robert A. Wagner and Michael J. Fischer. 1974. The string-to-string correction problem. *Journal of the Association for Computing Machinery*, 21(1):168–173.

Richard Wicentowski. 2004. Multilingual noise-robust supervised morphological analysis using the wordframe model. In *Proceedings of the 7th Meeting of the ACL Special Interest Group in Computational Phonology*, pages 70–77, Barcelona, Spain.

John U. Wolff. 1972. *A Dictionary of Cebuano Visaya*. Southeast Asia Program, Cornell University, Ithaca, New York.

Learning Probabilistic Paradigms for Morphology in a Latent Class Model

Erwin Chan
Dept. of Computer and Information Science
University of Pennsylvania
Philadelphia, PA 19104
echan3@seas.upenn.edu

Abstract

This paper introduces the *probabilistic paradigm*, a probabilistic, declarative model of morphological structure. We describe an algorithm that recursively applies Latent Dirichlet Allocation with an orthogonality constraint to discover morphological paradigms as the latent classes within a suffix-stem matrix. We apply the algorithm to data preprocessed in several different ways, and show that when suffixes are distinguished for part of speech and allomorphs or gender/conjugational variants are merged, the model is able to correctly learn morphological paradigms for English and Spanish. We compare our system with Linguistica (Goldsmith 2001), and discuss the advantages of the probabilistic paradigm over Linguistica's signature representation.

1 Introduction

In recent years researchers have addressed the task of unsupervised learning of declarative representations of morphological structure. These models include the signature of (Goldsmith 2001), the conflation set of (Schone and Jurafsky 2001), the paradigm of (Brent et. al. 2002), and the inflectional class of (Monson 2004). While these representations group morphologically related words in systematic ways, they are rather different from the paradigm, the representation of morphology in traditional grammars. A paradigm lists the prototypical morphological properties of lexemes belonging to a particular part of speech (POS) category; for example, a paradigm for regular English verbs would include the suffixes {$,ed$,ing$,s$}[1]. Hand-built computational implementations of paradigms as inheritance hierarchies include DATR (Evans and Gazdar 1996) and Functional Morphology (Forsberg and Ranta 2004). The two principal ways in which learned models have differed from paradigms are that: 1) they do not have POS types, and 2) they are not abstractions that generalize beyond the words of the input corpus.

There are important reasons for learning a POS-associated, paradigmatic representation of morphology. Currently, the dominant technology for morphological analysis involves mapping between inflected and base of forms of words with finite-state transducers (FSTs), a procedural model of morphological relations. Rewrite rules are handcrafted and compiled into FSTs, and it would be beneficial if these rules could be learned automatically. One line of research in computational morphology has been directed towards learning finite-state mapping rules from some sort of paradigmatic structure, where all morphological forms and POS types are presumed known for a set of lexemes (Clark 2001, Kazakov and Manandhar 2001, Oflazer et. al. 2001, Zajac 2001, Albright 2002). This can be accomplished by first deciding on a base form, then learning rules to convert other forms of the paradigm into this base form. If one could develop an unsupervised algorithm for learning paradigms, it could serve as the input to rule-learning procedures, effectively leading to an entirely unsupervised system for learning FSTs from raw data. This is our long-term goal.

[1] $ is the null suffix.

Proceedings of the Eighth Meeting of the ACL Special Interest Group on Computational Phonology at HLT-NAACL 2006, pages 69–78,
New York City, USA, June 2006.

An alternative approach is to skip the paradigm formulation step and construct a procedural model directly from raw data. (Yarowsky and Wicentowski 2000) bootstrap inflected and base forms directly from raw data and learn mappings between them. Their results are quite successful, but the morphological information they learn is not structured as clearly as a paradigmatic model. (Freitag 2005) constructs a morphological automaton, where nodes are clustered word types and arcs are suffixation rules.

This paper addresses the problem of finding an organization of stems and suffixes as probabilistic paradigms (section 2), a model of morphology closer to linguistic notion of paradigm than previously proposed models. We encode the morphological structure of a language in a matrix containing frequencies of words, and formulate the problem of learning paradigms as one of finding latent classes within the matrix. We present a recursive LDA, a learning algorithm based on Latent Dirichlet Allocation (section 3), and show that under certain conditions (section 5), it can correctly learn morphological paradigms for English and Spanish. In section 6, we compare the probabilistic paradigm to the signature model of (Goldsmith 2001). In section 7, we sketch some ideas for how to make our system more unsupervised and more linguistically adequate.

We assume a model of morphology where each word is the concatenation of a stem and a single suffix representing all of the word's morphological and POS properties. Although this is a very simplistic view of morphology, there are many hitherto unresolved computational issues for learning even this basic model, and we consider it necessary to address these issues before developing more sophisticated models. For a stem/suffix representation, the task of learning a paradigm from raw data involves proposing suffixes and stems, proposing segmentations, and systematically organizing stems and suffixes into classes. One difficulty is suffix allomorphy: a suffix has multiple forms depending on its phonological environment (e.g. `s$/es$`). Another problem is suffix categorial ambiguity (`s$` is ambiguous for noun and verb uses). Finally, lexemes appear in only a subset of their potential forms, due to sparse data. An unsupervised learner needs to be able to handle all of these difficulties in order to discover abstract paradigmatic classes.

In this paper, we are primarily interested in how the co-occurrence of stems and suffixes in a corpus leads them to be organized into paradigms. We use data preprocessed with correct segmentations of words into stems and suffixes, in order to focus on the issue of determining what additional knowledge is needed. We demonstrate that paradigms for English and Spanish can be successfully learned when tokens have been assigned POS tags and allomorphs or gender/conjugational variants are given a common representation. Our learning algorithm is not supervised since the target concept of gold standard "input" POS category of stems is not known, but rather it is an unsupervised algorithm that relies on preprocessed data for optimal performance.

2 The Probabilistic Paradigm

We introduce the *probabilistic paradigm*, a probabilistic, declarative model of regular morphology. The probabilistic paradigm model consists of three matrices: the data matrix D, the morphological probabilities matrix M, and the lexical probabilities matrix L. Let `m` be the number of stems, `n` the number of stems, and `p` the number of paradigms. The D matrix encodes the joint distribution of lexical and morphological information in a corpus. It is of size `m x n`, and each cell contains the frequency of the word formed by concatenating the appropriate stem and suffix. The M matrix is of size `m x p`, and each column contains the conditional probabilities of each suffix given a paradigm. The L matrix is of size `p x n`, and contains the conditional probabilities of each paradigm given a stem. Each suffix should belong to exactly one paradigm, and the suffixes of a particular paradigm should be conditionally independent. Each column of the M matrix defines a *canonical paradigm*, a set of suffixes that attach to stems associated with that paradigm. A *lexical paradigm* is the full set of word forms for a particular stem, and is an instantiation of the canonical paradigm for a particular stem.

The probabilistic paradigm is not well-developed as the usual notion of "paradigm" in linguistics. First, the system employs no labels such as "noun", "plural", "past", etc. Second, probabilistic paradigms have only a top-level categorization; induced "verb" paradigms, for example, are not substructured into different tenses or conjugations. Third, we do not distinguish between inflectional and derivational morphology; traditional grammars place derived forms in separate lexical paradigms. Fourth, we do not handle syncretism, where one suffix belongs in multiple slots of the paradigm. Fifth, we do not yet not handle irregular and sub-regular forms. Despite these drawbacks, our paradigms have an important advantage over traditional paradigms, in being probabilistic and therefore able to model language usage.

3 Learning the probabilistic paradigm in a latent class model

We learn the parameters of the probabilistic paradigm model by applying a dimensionality reduction algorithm to the D matrix, in order to produce the M and L matrices. This reduces the size of the representation from `m*n` to `m*p + p*n`. The main idea is to discover the latent classes (paradigms) which represent the underlying structure of the input matrix. This handles two important problems: 1) that words occur in a subset of their possible morphological forms in a corpus, and 2) that the words formed from a particular stem can belong to multiple POS categories. The second problem can be quantified as follows: in our English data, 14.3% of types occur with multiple open-class base POS categories, accounting for 56.5% of tokens; for Spanish, 13.7% of types, 37.8% of tokens.

3.1 LDA model for morphology

The dimensionality reduction algorithm that we employ is Latent Dirichlet Allocation (LDA) (Blei et. al. 2003). LDA is a generative probabilistic model for discrete data. For the application of topic discovery within a corpus of documents, a document consists of a mixture of underlying topics, and each topic consists of a probability distribution over the vocabulary. The topic proportions are drawn from a Dirichlet distribution, and the words are drawn from a multinomial over the topic. Probability distributions of documents and words are conditionally independent of topics. LDA produces two non-negative parameter matrices, Gamma and Beta: Gamma is the matrix of Dirichlet posteriors, encoding the distribution of documents and topics; Beta encodes the distribution of words and topics.

The mapping of the data structures of LDA to the probabilistic paradigm is as follows. The document-word matrix is analogous to the suffix-stem D matrix. For morphology, a "document" is a multiset of tokens in a corpus, such that each of those tokens decomposes into a stem and a specified suffix. Different underlying canonical paradigms ("topics") can be associated with suffixes, and each canonical paradigm allows a set of stems ("words"). For a suffix-stem ("document-word") matrix of size `m x n` and `k` latent classes, the Gamma matrix is of size `m x k`, and the Beta matrix is of size `k x n`. The Gamma matrix, normalized by column, is the M matrix, and the Beta matrix, normalized by row, is the L matrix.

3.2 Recursive LDA

One standard issue in using these types of algorithms is selecting the number of classes. To deal with this, we have formulated a recursive wrapper algorithm for LDA that accomplishes a divisive clustering of suffixes. LDA is run at each stage to find the local Gamma and Beta matrices. To split the suffixes into two classes, we assign each suffix to the class for which its probability is greater, by examining the Gamma matrix. The input matrix is then divided into two smaller matrices based on this split, and the algorithm continues with each submatrix. The result is a binary tree describing the suffix splits at each node.

To construct a classification of suffixes into paradigms, it is necessary to make a cut in the tree. Assuming that suffix splits are optimal, we start at the root of the tree and go down until reaching a node where there is sufficient uncertainty about which class a suffix should belong to. A good split of suffixes is one where the vectors of probabilities of suffixes given a class are orthogonal; we can find such a split by minimizing the cosine of the two columns of the node's Gamma matrix (we call this the "Gamma cosine"). Thus, a node at which suffixes should not be split has a high Gamma cosine, and when encountering such a node, a cut should be made. The suffixes below this node are grouped together as a paradigm; tree structure below the cut node is ignored. In our experiments we have selected thresholds for the Gamma cosine, but we do not know if there is a single value that would be successful cross-linguistically. After the tree has been cut, the Gamma and Beta matrices for ancestor nodes are normalized and combined to form the M and L matrices for the language.

Another issue is dealing with suboptimal solutions. Random initializations of parameters lead the EM training procedure to local maxima in the solution space, and as a result LDA produces differing suffix splits across different runs. To get around this, we simply run LDA multiple times (25 in our experiments) and choose the solution that minimizes the Gamma cosine.

We also experimented with minimizing the Beta cosine. The Beta matrix represents stem ambiguity with respect to a suffix split. Since there are inherently ambiguous stems, one should not expect the Beta cosine value to be extremely low. Minimizing the Beta cosine sometimes made the Beta matrix "too disambiguated" and forced the representation of ambiguity into Gamma matrix, thereby inflating the Gamma cosine and causing incorrect classifications of suffixes.

4 Data

We conducted experiments on English and Spanish. For English, we chose the Penn Treebank (Marcus et. al. 1993), which is already POS-tagged; for Spanish, we chose an equivalent-sized portion of newswire (Graff and Galegos 1999), POS-tagged by the FreeLing morphological analyzer (Carreras et. al. 2004). We restricted our data to nouns, verbs, adjectives, and adverbs. Words that did not follow canonical suffixation patterns for their POS category (irregulars, foreign words, incorrectly tagged words, etc.) were excluded. We segmented each word into stem and suffix for a specified set of suffixes. Rare suffixes were excluded, such as many English adjective-forming suffixes and Spanish 2nd person plural forms. Stems were not lemmatized, with the result that there can be multiple stem variants of a particular lemma, as with the words `stemm.ing$` and `stem.s$`. Tokens were not disambiguated for word sense. Stems that occurred with only one suffix were excluded.

We use several different representations of suffixes in constructing the data matrices: 1) merged, labeled suffixes; 2) merged, unlabeled suffixes; 3) unmerged, unlabeled suffixes. For unmerged suffixes, allomorphs[2] are represented in their original spelling. A merged suffix is a common representation for the multiple surface manifestations of an underlyingly identical suffix. Suffixes also can be unlabeled, or labeled with base POS tags. For an example, a verb `created` would be segmented as `create.d$` with an unmerged, labeled suffix, or `create.d/ed$V` with a merged, labeled suffix. Labels disambiguate otherwise categorically ambiguous suffixes.

The gold standard for each language lists the suffixes that belong to a paradigm for stems of a particular POS category. We call this the "input" POS category, which is not indicated in annotations and is the concept to be predicted. This should be differentiated from the "output" POS labels on the suffixes: for example, `ly$R` attaches to stems of the input category "adjective". Each suffix is an atomic entity, so the system actually has no concept of output POS categories. All that we require is that distinct suffixes are given distinct symbols.

In the English gold standard (Table 1), each slashed pair of suffixes denotes one merged form; the unmerged forms are the individual suffixes. `ally$R` is the suffix `ly$R` preceded by an epenthetic vowel, as in the word `basically`. In the Spanish gold standard (Table 2), each slashed group of suffixes corresponds to one merged form. For adjectives and nouns, `a$` and `o$` are feminine and masculine singular forms, and `as$` and `os$` are the corresponding plurals. `$` and `s$` do not have gender; `es$` is a plural allomorph. `mente/amente$R` is a derivational suffix. The first two groups of verbal suffixes are past participles, agreeing in number and gender. For the other verb forms, when three are listed they correspond to forms for the 1st, 2nd, and 3rd conjugations. When there are two, the first is for the 1st conjugation, and the other is identical for the 2nd and 3rd. `o$V` has the same form across all three conjugations.

Adjectives:	`$A, d/ed$A, r/er$A, ally/ly$R`
Nouns:	`$N, 's$N, es/s$N`
Verbs:	`$V, d/ed$V, es/s$V, ing$V, ing$A, ing$N, r/er$N`

Table 1. Gold standard for English

[2] We abuse the standard usage of the term "allomorph" to include gender and conjugational variants.

Adjectives:	a/o/$A, as/os/es/s$A, mente/amente$R
Nouns:	a/o/$N, as/os/es/s$N
Verbs:	ada/ida/ado/ido$V, adas/idas/ados/idos$V, ando/iendo$V, ar/er/ir$V, o$V, as/es$V, a/e$V, amos/emos/imos$V, an/en$V, aba/ía$V, ábamos/íamos$V, aban/ían$V, aré/eré/iré$V, ará/erá/irá$V, aremos/eremos/iremos$V, arán/erán/irán$V, é/í$V, ó/ió$V, aron/ieron$V, aría/ería/iría$V, arían/erían/irían$V

Table 2. Gold standard for Spanish

5 Experiments

5.1 Merged, labeled suffixes

Figure 1 shows the recursion tree for English data preprocessed with merged, labeled suffixes. To produce a classification of suffixes into paradigms, we start at the root and go down until reaching nodes with a Gamma cosine greater than or equal to the threshold. The cut for a threshold of .0009 produces three paradigms exactly matching the gold standard for verbs, adjectives, and nouns, respectively. Table 3 shows the complete M matrix, which contains suffix probabilities for each paradigm. Table 4 shows a portion of the L matrix, which contains the probabilities of stems belonging to paradigms. We list the stems that are most ambiguous with respect to paradigm membership (note that this table does not specify the *words* that belong to each category, only their *stems*).

	"Verb"	"Adj"	"Noun"
$A	0.000	0.829	0.000
d/ed$A	0.020	0.000	0.000
r/er$A	0.000	0.033	0.000
ing$A	0.008	0.000	0.000
$N	0.000	0.000	0.706
's$N	0.000	0.000	0.036
r/er$N	0.037	0.000	0.000
ing$N	0.065	0.000	0.000
es/s$N	0.000	0.000	0.257
ally/ly$R	0.000	0.138	0.000
$V	0.342	0.000	0.000
d/ed$V	0.284	0.000	0.000
ing$V	0.133	0.000	0.000
es/s$V	0.110	0.000	0.000

Table 3. M matrix for English merged, labeled suffixes. Columns: p(suff|paradigm).

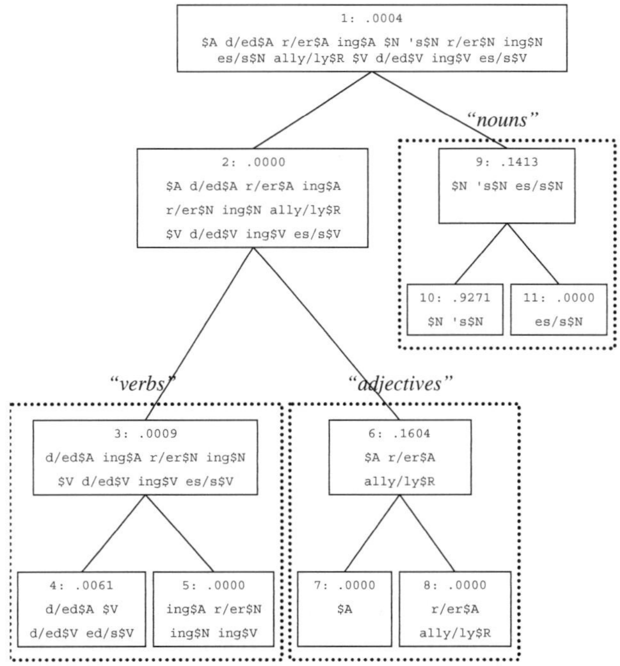

Figure 1. Recursion tree for English merged, labeled suffixes. Each node shows its current suffix set, and the Gamma cosine value for the split. Dotted lines indicate paradigms for a Gamma cosine threshold of .0009.

	"Verb"	"Adj"	"Noun"
reset	0.333	0.292	0.375
blunt	0.445	0.278	0.277
calm	0.417	0.375	0.209
total	0.312	0.462	0.226
clean	0.478	0.319	0.203
parallel	0.222	0.278	0.500
alert	0.500	0.222	0.277
sound	0.483	0.184	0.333
compound	0.372	0.171	0.457
pale	0.417	0.417	0.166
fine	0.254	0.230	0.516
premier	0.235	0.235	0.529
brief	0.175	0.524	0.301
polish	0.250	0.556	0.194
ski	0.378	0.108	0.513
fake	0.200	0.600	0.200
light	0.092	0.427	0.481
foster	0.226	0.161	0.613
bottom	0.107	0.304	0.589
repurchase	0.333	0.095	0.571

Table 4. Portion of L matrix for English merged, labeled suffixes, sorted by lowest entropy. Columns: p(paradigm|stem).

Next, we examine the morphological and lexical conditional probabilities in the M and L matrices. It is possible that even though the correct classification of suffixes into paradigms was learned, the probabilities may be off. Table 5 shows, however, that the M and L matrices are an extremely accurate approximation of the true morphological and lexical probabilities. We have included statistics for the corresponding Spanish experiment; the paradigms that were discovered for Spanish also match the gold standard.

	English	Spanish
# suffixes	14	26
# stems	7315	5115
CRE M	.0002 bits	.0003 bits
CRE L	.0006 bits	.0020 bits

Table 5. Comparison of M and L matrices with true morphological and lexical probabilities, by conditional relative entropy (CRE).

5.2 Unmerged, labeled suffixes

The next experiments tested the effect of allomorphy on paradigm discovery, using data where suffixes are labeled but not merged. There are competing pressures at work in determining how allomorphs are assigned to paradigms: on the one hand, the disjointedness of stem sets for allomorphs would tend to place them in separate paradigms; on the other hand, if those stem sets have other suffixes in common that belong to the same paradigm, the allomorphs might likewise be placed in that paradigm. In our experiments, we found that there was much more variability across runs than in the merged suffix cases. In English, for example, the suffix es$N was sometimes placed in the "verb" paradigm, although the maximally orthogonal solution placed it in the "noun" paradigm.

Figure 2 shows the recursion tree and paradigms for Spanish. Gold standard noun and adjective categories are fragmented into multiple paradigms in the tree. Although nouns have a common parent node (2), the nouns of the different genders are placed in separate paradigms -- this is because a noun can have only one gender. The verbs are all in a single paradigm (node 10). Node 11 contains all the first-conjugation verbs, and node 12 contains all the second/third-conjugation verbs. The reason that they are not in separate paradigms is that a$V is shared by stems of all three conjugations, which leads to a split that is not quite orthogonal.

The case of adjectives is the most interesting. Gendered and non-gendered adjective stems are disjoint, so adjectives appear in two separate subtrees (nodes 4, 13). In node 4, the gender-ambiguous plural es$A is in conflict with the plural s$A, but it would conflict with two plurals as$A and os$A if it were placed in node 13. amente$R appears together in node 14 because it shares stems with the feminine adjectives. amente$R also shares stems with verbs, as it is also the derivational suffix which attaches to verbal past participles in the feminine "a" form. This is probably why the group of adjectives at node 13 is a sister to the verb nodes. The allomorph mente$R attaches to non-gendered adjectives, and is thus in the first adjective group.

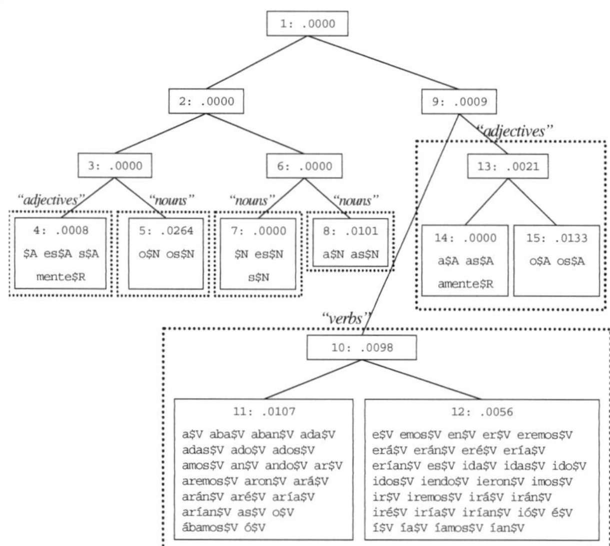

Figure 2. Recursion tree for Spanish, unmerged, labeled suffixes, with Gamma cosine values. Dotted lines indicate paradigms for a Gamma cosine threshold of .0021.

5.3 Unmerged, unlabeled suffixes

The case of unmerged, unlabeled suffixes is not as successful. In the Gamma matrix for the root node (Table 6), there is no orthogonal division of the suffixes, as indicated by the high Gamma cosine value of .1705. Despite this, the algorithm has discovered useful information. There is a subparadigm of unambiguous suffixes {'s$,ally$}, and another of {d$,ed$,ing$,r$}. The other suffixes ($,er$,es$,ly$,s$) are ambiguous. The ambiguity of ly$ seems to be a secondary effect: since adjectives with the null suffix $ are found to be ambiguous, ly$ is likewise ambiguous.

$	[0.9055]	0.0703
's$	[0.0351]	0.0000
ally$	[0.0007]	0.0000
d$	0.0000	[0.1139]
ed$	0.0000	[0.1332]
er$	[0.0087]	0.0084
es$	[0.0089]	0.0001
ing$	0.0000	[0.1176]
ly$	0.0033	[0.0603]
r$	0.0000	[0.0198]
s$	0.0378	[0.4764]

Table 6. Gamma matrix for root node, English, unmerged, unlabeled suffixes; the categorization is shown with brackets. Columns indicate p(suffix|class).

6 Comparison with Linguistica

In this section, we compare our system with Linguistica[3] (Goldsmith 2001), a freely available program for unsupervised discovery of morphological structure. We focus our attention on Linguistica's representation of morphology, rather than the algorithm used to learn it. Linguistica takes a list of word types, proposes segmentations of words into stems and suffixes, and organizes them into signatures. A *signature* is a non-probabilistic data structure that groups together all stems that share a common set of suffixes. Each stem belongs to exactly one signature, and the set of suffixes for each signature is unique. For example, running Linguistica on our raw English text, there is a signature {$,ful$,s$} for the stems {resource, truth, youth}, indicating the morphology of the words {resource$, truth$, youth$, resourceful$, truthful$, youthful$, resources$, truths$, youths$}. There are no POS types in the system. Thus, even for a prototypically "noun" signature such as {$,'s$}, it is quite possible that not all of the words that the signature represents are actually nouns. For example, the word structure$ is in this signature, but occurs both as a noun (59 times) and a verb (2 times) in our corpus.

The signature model can be derived from the suffix-stem data matrix, by first converting all positive counts to 1, and then placing in separate groups all the stems that have the same 0/1 column pattern. Another way to view the signature is as a special case of the probabilistic paradigm where all probabilities are restricted to being 0 or 1, for if this were so, the only way to fit the data would be to let there be a canonical paradigm for every different subset of suffixes that some stem appears with. In theory, it is possible for the number of signatures to be exponential in the number of suffixes; in practice, Linguistica finds hundreds of signatures for English and Spanish. Although there has been work on reducing the number of signatures (Goldwater and Johnson 2004; Hu et. al. 2005, who report a reduction of up to 30%), the number of remaining signatures is still two orders of magnitude greater than the number of canonical paradigms we find. The simplest explanation for this is that a suffix can be listed many times in the different signatures, but only has one entry in the M matrix of the probabilistic paradigm.

It is important for a natural language system to handle out-of-vocabulary words. A signature does not predict the forms of potential but unseen forms of stems. To some extent Linguistica could accommodate this, as it identifies when one signature's suffixes are a proper subset of another's, but it does not handle cases where suffixes are partially overlapping. One principal advantage of the probabilistic paradigm is that the canonical paradigm allows the instantiation of a lexical paradigm containing a complete set of predicted word forms for a stem.

Since Linguistica is a system that starts from raw text, it may seem that it cannot be directly compared to our work, which assumes that segmentations and suffixes are already known. However, it is possible to run Linguistica on our data by doing further preprocessing. We rewrite the corpus in such a way that Linguistica can detect correct morphological and POS information for each token. Each token is replaced by the concatenation of its stem, the dummy string 12345, and a single-character encoding of its merged suffix. For example, the token accelerate.d/ed$V is mapped to accelerate12345D, where D represents d/ed$V. The omnipresence of the dummy string enables

[3] http://linguistica.uchigago.edu

Linguistica to discover all the desired stems and suffixes, but no more. By mapping the input corpus in this way, we can examine the type of grammar that Linguistica would find if it knew the information that we have assumed in the previous experiments. Linguistica found 565 signatures from the "cooked" English data (Figure 3). 50% of word types are represented by the first 13 signatures.

```
1. { $N, es/s$N } 1540
   abortion absence accent acceptance
   accident accolade accommodation
2. { $N, 's$N } 1168
   aba abbie abc academy achenbaum aclu
   adams addington addison adobe
3. { $N, 's$N, es/s$N } 224
   accountant acquisition actor
   administration airline airport alliance
5. { $A, ally/ly$R } 319
   abrupt absolute abundant accurate
   actual additional adequate adroit
6. { $A, $N, es/s$N } 173
   abrasive acid activist adhesive adult
   afghan african afrikaner aggregate
7. { $V, d/ed$V, es/s$V } 135
   abate achieve administer afflict
   aggravate alienate amass apologize
9. { $V, d/ed$V, ing$V, es/s$V } 73
   abound absorb adopt applaud assert
   assist attend attract avert avoid
13. { $N, $V, d/ed$V, es/s$N, es/s$V } 44
    advocate amount attribute battle
    bounce cause compromise decline
```

Figure 3. Selected top signatures for merged, labeled suffix English data. Each signature shows the suffix set, number of stems, and several example stems. Ranking is by `log(num stems)* log(num suffixes)`.

We have formulated two metrics to evaluate the quality of a collection of signatures or paradigms. Ideally, all suffixes of a particular signature would be of the same category, and all the words of a particular category would be contained within one signature. *POS fragmentation* measures to what extent the words of an input POS category are scattered across different signatures. It is the average number of bits required to encode the probability distribution of some category's words over signatures. *Signature impurity* measures the extent to which the suffixes of a signature are of mixed input POS types. It is the expected value of the number of bits required to encode the probability distribution of some signature's suffixes over input POS categories. Table 7 shows that, according to these metrics, the signature does not organize morphological information as efficiently as probabilistic paradigms[4]. Linguistica's impurity scores are reasonably low because many of the signatures with the most stems are categorically homogeneous. Fragmentation scores show that the placement of the majority of words within top signatures offsets the scattering of a POS category's suffixes over many signatures.

(1) POS fragmentation =

$$\left[\sum_{P} h(p(\mathrm{S} \mid \text{words of P}))\right] \Big/ |\mathrm{P}|$$

(2) Signature impurity =

$$\left[\sum_{S} \mathrm{S.numstems} \times h(p(\mathrm{P} \mid \mathrm{S}))\right] \Big/ \sum_{S} \mathrm{S.numstems}$$

h: entropy
P: input POS categories
S: signatures / paradigms

	Linguistica	Recursive LDA
English fragmentation	5.422 bits	0 bits
English impurity	.404 bits	0 bits
Spanish fragmentation	6.084 bits	0 bits
Spanish impurity	.332 bits	0 bits

Table 7. Comparison of Linguistica and recursive LDA on merged, labeled suffix data. The maximum possible impurity for 3 POS categories is $log_2(3) = 1.585$ bits.

Finally, a morphological grammar should reflect the general, abstract morphological structure of the language from which a corpus was sampled. To test for consistency of morphological grammars across corpora, we split our cooked English data into two equal parts. Linguistica found 449 total signatures for the first half and 462 for the second. 296 signatures were common to both (in terms of the suffixes contained by the signatures). Of the 3506 stems shared by both data sets, 1831 (52.2%) occurred in the same signature. Of the top 50 signatures for each half-corpus, 45 were in common, and 1651 of 2403 shared stems (68.7%) occurred in the same signature. Recursive LDA found the

[4] Our scores would not be so good if we had chosen a poor Gamma cosine threshold value for classification. However, Linguistica's scores cannot be decreased, as there is only one signature model for a fixed set of stems and suffixes.

same canonical paradigms for both data sets (which matched the gold standard). Differences in word counts between the corpus halves altered stem inventories and lexical probabilities, but not the structure of the canonical paradigms. Our system thus displays a robustness to corpus choice that does not hold for Linguistica.

7 Future Work

This section sketches some ideas for future work to increase the linguistic adequacy of the system, and to make it more unsupervised.

1. Bootstrapping: for fully unsupervised learning, we need to hypothesize stems and suffixes. The output of recursive LDA indicates which suffixes may be ambiguous. To bootstrap a disambiguator for the different categorial uses of these suffixes, one could use various types of distributional information, as well as knowledge of partial paradigmatic structure for non-ambiguous suffixes.
2. Automated detection of cut nodes: currently the system requires that the user select a Gamma cosine threshold for extracting paradigms from the recursion tree. We would like to automate this process, perhaps with different heuristics.
3. Suffix merging and formulation of generation rules: when we decide that two suffixes should be merged (based on some measures of distributional similarity and word-internal context), we also need to formulate phonological (i.e., spelling) rules to determine which surface form to use when instantiating a form from the canonical paradigm.
4. Non-regular forms: we can take advantage of empty cells in the data matrix in order to identify non-regularities such as suppletives, stem variants, semi-regular subclasses, and suffix allomorphs. If the expected frequency of a word form (as derived from the M matrix and frequency of a stem) is relatively high but the value in the D matrix is zero, this is evidence that a non-regular form may occupy this cell. Locating irregular words could use methods similar to those of (Yarowsky and Wicentowski 2000), who pair irregular inflections and their roots from raw text. Stem variants and allomorphic suffixes could be detected in a similar manner, by finding sets of stems/suffixes with mutually exclusive matrix entries.
5. Multiple morphological properties per word: we currently represent all morphological and POS information with a single suffix. The learning algorithm and representation could perhaps be modified to allow for multiple morphological properties. One could perform recursive LDA on a particular morphological property, then take each of the learned paradigms and perform recursive LDA again, but for a different morphological property. This method might discover Spanish conjugational classes as subclasses within "verbs".

8 Discussion

This paper has introduced the probabilistic paradigm model of morphology. It has some important benefits: it is an abstract, compact representation of a language's morphology, it accommodates lexical ambiguity, and it predicts forms of words not seen in the input data.

We have formulated the problem of learning probabilistic paradigms as one of discovering latent classes within a suffix-stem count matrix, through the recursive application of LDA with an orthogonality constraint. Under optimal data conditions, it can learn the correct paradigms, and also models morphological and lexical probabilities extremely accurately. It is robust to corpus choice, so we can say that it learns a morphological grammar for the *language*. This is a new application of matrix factorization algorithms, and an usual one: whereas in document topic modeling, one tries to find that a document consists of multiple topics, we want to find orthogonal decompositions where each suffix (document) belongs to only one input POS category (topic).

We have demonstrated that the algorithm can successfully learn morphological paradigms for English and Spanish under the conditions that segmentations are known, categorically ambiguous suffixes have been distinguished, and allomorphs have been merged. When suffixes have not been merged, there is a tendency to place allomorphic variants in different paradigms. The algorithm is the least successful in the unmerged, unlabeled case, as ambiguous suffixes do not allow for a clear split of suffixes into paradigms. However, the program output indicates which suffixes are potentially ambiguous or unambiguous, and this information could be used by bootstrapping procedures for suffix disambiguation.

Some of the behavior of the learning algorithm can be explained in terms of several constraints. First, LDA assumes conditional independence of documents (suffixes) given topics (paradigms). A stem should be able to occur with each suffix of a canonical paradigm. But if a stem occurs with one allomorphic variant of a suffix, we know that it necessarily cannot occur with the other. Therefore, allomorphy violates conditional independence of suffixes given a paradigm, and we cope with this by merging allomorphs. Second, LDA also assumes conditional independence of words (stems) given topics (paradigm). As our data contains stem variants, this assumption does not hold either, but it is a less serious violation due to the large number of total stems. Third, we have imposed the constraint of orthogonality of suffixes and paradigms, which is not required by LDA (and actually undesired in document topic modeling, since documents can contain multiple topics). Orthogonal suffix splits are possible when categorically ambiguous suffixes have been disambiguated.

In conclusion, we view morphology learning as a process of manipulating the representation of data to fit a learnable computational model. The alternative would be to complicate the model and learning algorithm to accommodate raw data and all its concurrent ambiguities and dependencies. We hypothesize that successful, fully unsupervised learning of linguistically adequate representations of morphology will be more easily accomplished by first bootstrapping the sorts of information that we have assumed, or, in other words, fitting the data to the model.

Acknowledgements

This work was supported by the National Science Foundation under grant NSF IIS-0415138. The author thanks Mitch Marcus and anonymous reviewers for their helpful comments.

References

A. Albright. 2002. The identification of bases in morphological paradigms. Ph.D. thesis, UCLA.

D. Blei, A. Ng, and M. Jordan. 2003. Latent dirichlet allocation. Journal of Machine Learning Research 3, 993-1022.

X. Carreras, I. Chao, L. Padró, and M. Padró. 2004. FreeLing: an open-source suite of language analyzers. Proceedings of LREC. Lisbon, Portugal.

A. Clark. 2001. Learning morphology with pair hidden markov models. Proceedings of the Student Workshop at ACL.

R. Evans and G. Gazdar. 1996. DATR: A language for lexical knowledge representation. Computational Linguistics 22(2), 167-216.

M. Forsberg and A. Ranta. 2004. Functional morphology. Proceedings of the ICFP, 213-223. ACM Press.

D. Freitag. 2005. Morphology induction from term clusters. Proceedings of CoNLL.

J. Goldsmith. 2001. Unsupervised learning of the morphology of a natural language. Computational Linguistics 27(2), 153-198.

S. Goldwater and M. Johnson. 2004. Priors in bayesian learning of phonological rules. Proceedings of SIGPHON.

D. Graff and G. Gallegos. 1999. Spanish newswire text, volume 2. Linguistic Data Consortium, Philadelphia, PA.

Y. Hu, I. Matveeva, J. Goldsmith, and C. Sprague. 2005. Using morphology and syntax together in unsupervised learning. Workshop on Psychocomputational Models of Human Language Acquisition.

D. Kazakov and S. Manandhar. 2001. Unsupervised learning of word segmentation rules with genetic algorithms and inductive logic programming. Machine Learning 43, 121-162.

M. Marcus, B. Santorini and M.A. Marcinkiewicz. 1993. Building a large annotated corpus of English: The Penn Treebank. Computational Linguistics 19(2), 313-330.

C. Monson, A. Lavie, J. Carbonell, and L. Levin. 2004. Unsupervised induction of natural language morphology inflection classes. Proc. of SIGPHON.

K. Oflazer, S. Nirenburg, and M. McShane. 2001. Bootstrapping morphological analyzers by combining human elicitation and machine learning. Computational Linguistics 27(1), 59-85.

P. Schone and D. Jurafsky. 2001. Knowledge-free induction of inflectional morphologies. Proc. NAACL.

M. Snover, G. Jarosz, and M. Brent. 2002. Unsupervised learning of morphology using a novel directed search algorithm: taking the first step. Proceedings of SIGPHON.

D. Yarowsky and R. Wicentowski. 2000. Minimally supervised morphological analysis by multimodal alignment. Proceedings of ACL.

R. Zajac. 2001. Morpholog: constrained and supervised learning of morphology. Proceedings of CoNLL.

A Naive Theory of Affixation and an Algorithm for Extraction

Harald Hammarström
Dept. of Computing Science
Chalmers University of Technology
412 96, Gothenburg Sweden
harald2@cs.chalmers.se

Abstract

We present a novel approach to the unsupervised detection of affixes, that is, to extract a set of salient prefixes and suffixes from an unlabeled corpus of a language. The underlying theory makes no assumptions on whether the language uses a lot of morphology or not, whether it is prefixing or suffixing, or whether affixes are long or short. It does however make the assumption that 1. salient affixes have to be frequent, i.e occur much more often that random segments of the same length, and that 2. words essentially are variable length sequences of random characters, e.g a character should not occur in far too many words than random without a reason, such as being part of a very frequent affix. The affix extraction algorithm uses only information from fluctation of frequencies, runs in linear time, and is free from thresholds and untransparent iterations. We demonstrate the usefulness of the approach with example case studies on typologically distant languages.

1 Introduction

The problem at hand can be described as follows:

Input : An unlabeled corpus of an arbitrary natural language

Output : A (possibly ranked) set of prefixes and suffixes corresponding to true prefixes and suffixes in the linguistic sense, i.e well-segmented and with grammatical meaning, for the language in question.

Restrictions : We consider only concatenative morphology and assume that the corpus comes already segmented on the word level.

The theory and practice of the problem is relevant or even essential in fields such as child language acquisition, information retrieval and, of course, the fuller scope of computational morphology and its further layers of application (e.g Machine Translation).

The reasons for attacking this problem in an unsupervised manner include advantages in elegance, economy of time and money (no annotated resources required), and the fact that the same technology may be used on new languages.

An outline of the paper is as follows: we start with some notation and basic definitions, with which we describe the theory that is intended to model the essential behaviour of affixation in natural languages. Then we describe in detail and with examples the thinking behind the affix extraction algorithm, which actually requires only a few lines to define mathematically. Next, we present and discuss some experimental results on typologically different languages. The paper then finishes with a brief but comprehensive characterization of related work and its differences to our work. At the very end we state the most important conclusions and ideas on future components of unsupervised morphological analysis.

Proceedings of the Eighth Meeting of the ACL Special Interest Group on Computational Phonology at HLT-NAACL 2006, pages 79–88,
New York City, USA, June 2006.

2 A Naive Theory of Affixation

Notation and definitions:

- $w, s, b, x, y, \ldots \in \Sigma^*$: lowercase-letter variables range over strings of some alphabet Σ and are variously called words, segments, strings, etc.

- $s \lhd w$: s is a terminal segment of the word w i.e there exists a (possibly empty) string x such that $w = xs$

- $W, S, \ldots \subseteq \Sigma^*$: capital-letter variables range over sets of words/strings/segments

- $f_W(s) = |\{w \in W | s \lhd w\}|$: the number of words in W with terminal segment s

- $S_W = \{s | s \lhd w \in W\}$: all terminal segments of the words in W

- $|\cdot|$: is overloaded to denote both the length of a string and the cardinality of a set

Assume we have two sets of random strings over some alphabet Σ:

- Bases $B = \{b_1, b_2, \ldots, b_m\}$

- Suffixes $S = \{s_1, s_2, \ldots, s_n\}$

Such that:

Arbitrary Character Assumption (ACA) Each character $c \in \Sigma$ should be equally likely in any word-position for any member of B or S.

Note that B and S need not be of the same cardinality and that any string, including the empty string, could end up belonging to both B and S. They need neither to be sampled from the same distribution; pace the requirement, the distributions from which B and S are drawn may differ in how much probability mass is given to strings of different lengths. For instance, it would not be violation if B were drawn from a a distribution favouring strings of length, say, 42 and S from a distribution with a strong bias for short strings.

Next, build a set of affixed words $W \subseteq \{bs | b \in B, s \in S\}$, that is, a large set whose members are concatenations of the form bs for $b \in B, s \in S$, such that:

Frequent Flyer Assumption (FFA) : The members of S are frequent. Formally: Given any $s \in S$: $f_W(s) >> f_W(x)$ for all x such that 1. $|x| = |s|$; and 2. not $x \lhd s'$ for all $s' \in S$).

In other words, if we call $s \in S$ a *true suffix* and we call x an *arbitrary segment* if it neither a true suffix nor the terminal segment of a true suffix, then any true suffix should have much higher frequency than an arbitrary segment of the same length.

One may legimately ask to what extent words of real natural languages fit the construction model of W, with the strong ACA and FFA assumptions, outlined above. For instance, even though natural languages often aren't written phonemically, it is not hard to come up with languages that have phonotactic constraints on what may appear at the beginning or end of a word, e.g, Spanish **st-* may not begin a word and yields *est-* instead. Another violation of ACA is that (presumably all (Ladefoged, 2005)) languages disallow or disprefer a consonant vs. a vowel conditioned by the vowel/consonant status of its predecessor. However, if a certain element occurs with *less* frequency than random (the best example would be click consonants which, in some languages e.g Eastern !Xõo (Traill, 1994), occur only initially), this is not a problem to the theory.

As for FFA, we may have breaches such as Biblical Aramaic (Rosenthal, 1995) where an old *-ā* element appears on virtually everywhere on nouns, making it very frequent, but no longer has any synchronic meaning. Also, one can doubt the requirement that an affix should need to be frequent; for instance, the Classical Greek inflectional (lacking synchronic internal segmentation) alternative medial 3p. pl. aorist imperative ending -$\sigma\theta\omega\nu$ (Blomqvist and Jastrup, 1998), is not common at all.

Just how realistic the assumptions are is an empirical question, whose answer must be judged by experiments on the relevant languages. In the absense of fully annotated annotated test sets for diverse languages, and since the author does not have access to the Hutmegs/CELEX gold standard sets for Finnish and English (Creutz and Lindén, 2004), we can only give some guidelining experimental data.

ACA On a New Testament corpus of Basque (Leizarraga, 1571) we computed the probability of a character appearing in the initial, sec-

Positions	Distance
$\|\|p_1 - p_2\|\|$	0.47
$\|\|p_1 - p_3\|\|$	0.36
$\|\|p_1 - p_4\|\|$	0.37
$\|\|p_2 - p_3\|\|$	0.34
$\|\|p_2 - p_4\|\|$	0.23
$\|\|p_3 - p_4\|\|$	0.18

Table 1: Difference between character distributions according to word position.

ond, third or fourth position of the word. Since Basque is entirely suffixing, if it complied to ACA, we'd expect the distributions to be similar. However, if we look at the difference of the distributions in terms of variation distance between two probability distributions ($||p-q|| = \frac{1}{2}\sum_x |p(x) - q(x)|$), it shows that they differ considerably – especially the initial position proves more special (see table 1).

FFA As for the FFA, we checked a corpus of bible portions of Warlpiri (Yal, 1968 2001). This was chosen because it is one of the few languages known to the author where data was available and which has a decent amount of frequent suffixes which are also long, e.g case affixes are typically bisyllabic phonologically and five-ish characters long orthographically. Since the orthography used marked segmentation, it was easy to compute FFA statistics on the words as removed from segmentation marking. Comparing with the lists in (Nash, 1980, Ch. 2) it turns out that FFA is remarkably stable for all grammatical suffixes occuring in the outermost layer. There are however the expected kind of breaches; e.g a tense suffix *-ku* combined with a last vowel *-u* which is frequent in some frequent preceding affixes making the terminal segment *-uku* more frequent than some genuine three-letter suffixes.

The language known to the author which has shown the most systematic disconcord with the FFA is Haitian Creole (also in bible corpus experiments (Hai, 2003 1999)). Haitian creole has very little morphology of its own but owes the lion's share of it's words from French. French derivational morphemes abound in these words, e.g *-syon*, which have been carefully shown by (Lefebvre, 2004) not to be productive in Haitian Creole. Thus, the little morphology there is in Haitian creole is very difficult to get at without also getting the French relics.

3 An Algorithm for Affix Extraction

The key question is, if words in natural languages are constructed as W explained above, can we recover the segmentation? That is, can we find B and S, given only W? The answer is yes, we can partially decide this. To be more specific, we can compute a score Z such that $Z(x) > Z(y)$ if $x \in S_W$ and $y \notin S_W$. In general, the converse need not hold, i.e if both $x, y \in S_W$, or both $x, y \notin S_W$, then it may still be that $Z(x) > Z(y)$. This is equivalent to constructing a ranked list of all possible segments, where the true members of S_W appear at the top, and somewhere down the list the junk, i.e non-members of S_W, start appearing and fill up the rest of the list. Thus, it is not said *where* on the list the true-affixes/junk border begins, just that there is a consistent such border.

Now, how should this list be computed? Given the FFA, it's tempting to look at frequencies alone, i.e just go through all words and make a list of all segments, ranking them by frequency? This won't do it because 1. it doesn't compensate between segments of different length; naturally, short segments will be more frequent than long ones, solely by virtue of their shortness 2. it overcounts ill-segmented true affixes, e.g *-ng* will invariably get a higher (or equal) count than *-ing*. What we will do is a modification of this strategy, because 1. can easily be amended by subtracting estimated prior frequencies (under ACA) and there is a clever way of tackling 2. Note that, to amend 2., when going through w and each $s \lhd w$, it would be nice if we could count s only when it is well-segmented in w. We are given only W so this information is not available to us, but, the FFA assumption let's us make a local guess of it.

We shall illustrate the idea with an example of an evolving frequency curve of a word "playing" and its segmentations "playing", "aying", "ying", "ing", "ng", "g" (W being the set of words from an English bible corpus (Eng, 1977)). Figure 1 shows a

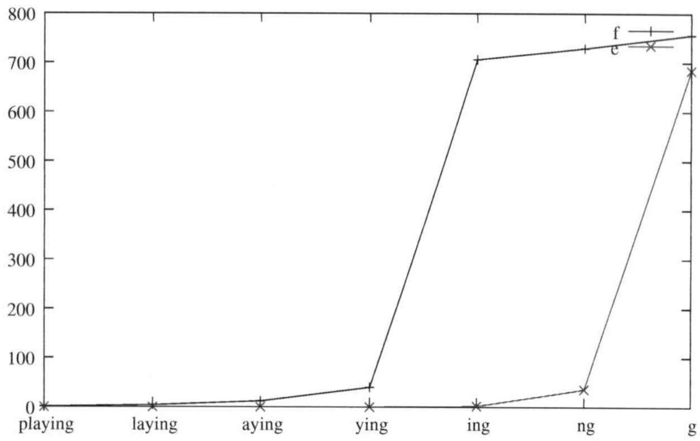

Figure 1: The observed $f_W(s)$ and expected $e_W(s)$ frequency for $s \lhd w = playing$.

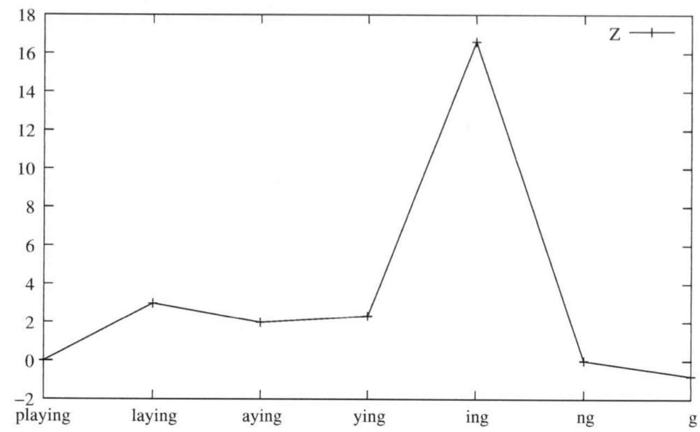

Figure 2: The slope of the $f'_W(s)$ curve for $s \lhd w = playing$.

frequency curve $f_W(s)$ and its expected frequency curve $e_W(s)$. The expected frequency of a suffix s doesn't depend on the actual characters of s and is defined as:

$$e_W(s) = |W| \cdot \frac{1}{r^{|s|}}$$

Where r is the size of the alphabet under the assumption that its characters are uniformly distributed. We don't simply use 26 in the case of lowercase English since not all characters are equally frequent. Instead we estimate the size of a would-be uniform distribution from the entropy of the distribution of the characters in W. This gives $r \approx 18.98$ for English and other languages with a similar writing practice.

Next, define the adjusted frequency as the difference between the observed frequency and the expected frequency:

$$f'_W(s) = f_W(s) - e_W(s)$$

It is the slope of this curve that predicts the presence of a good split. Figure 2 shows the appearance of this curve again exemplified by "playing".

After these examples, we are ready to define the segmentation score of a suffix relative to a word $Z : S_W \times W \to \mathbf{Q}$:

$$Z_W(s, w) = \begin{cases} 0 & \text{if not } s \lhd w \\ \frac{f'(s_i) - f'(s_{i-1})}{|f'(s_{i-1})|} & \text{if } s = s_i(w) \text{ for some} \end{cases}$$

Table 2 shows the evolution of exact values from the running example.

To move from a Z-score for a segment that is relative to a word we simply sum over all words to get the final score $Z : S_W \to \mathbf{Q}$:

$$Z_W(s) = \sum_{w \in W} Z(s, w) \tag{1}$$

To be extra clear, the FFA assumption is "exploited" in two ways. On the one hand, frequent affixes get many oppurtunities to get a score (which could, however, be negative) in the final sum over $w \in W$. On the other hand, the frequency is what make up the appearance of the slope that predicts the segmentation point.

The final Z-score in equation 1 is the one that purports to have the property that $Z(x) > Z(y)$ if $x \in S_W$ and $y \notin S_W$ – at least if purged (see below). A summary of the algorithm described in this section is displayed in table 3.

The time-complexity bounding factor is the number of suffixes, i.e the cardinality of S_W, which is linear (in the size of the input) if words are bounded in length by a constant and quadratic in the (really) worst case if not.

Input: A text corpus C

Step 1. Extract the set of words W from C (thus all contextual and word-frequency information is discarded)

Step 2. Calculate $Z_W(s, w)$ for each $w \in W$ and $s \lhd w$

Step 3. Accumulate $Z_W(s) = \sum_{w \in W} Z(s, w)$

Table 3: Summary of affix-extraction algorithm.

s	*playing*	*laying*	*aying*	*ying*	*ing*	*ng*	*g*
$f(s)$	1	4	12	40	706	729	756
$e_W(s)$	0.00	0.00	0.00	0.10	1.90	36.0	684
$f(s) - e_W(s)$	0.99	3.99	11.9	39.8	704	692	71.0
$Z(s,$"playing"$)$	**0.00**	**2.99**	**1.99**	**2.32**	**16.6**	**-0.0**	**-0.8**

Table 2: Exact values of frequency curves and scores from the running "playing" example.

1028682.0	*ing*	111264.0	*ling*
594208.0	*ed*	111132.0	*ent*
371145.0	*s*	109725.0	*ating*
337464.0	*'s*	109125.0	*ate*
326250.0	*ation*	108228.0	*an*
289536.0	*es*	97020.0	*ies*
238853.5	*e*	94560.0	*ts*
222256.0	*er*	81648.0	*ically*
191889.0	*ers*	81504.0	*ment*
172800.0	*ting*	78669.0	*led*
168288.0	*ly*	77900.0	*ering*
159408.0	*ations*	74976.0	*er's*
143775.0	*ted*	73988.0	*y*
130960.0	*able*	...	...
116352.0	*ated*	-26137.9	*l*
113364.0	*al*	-38620.6	*m*
113280.0	*ness*	-78757.3	*a*

Table 4: Top 30 and bottom 3 extracted suffixes for English. 47178 unique words yielded a total of 154407 ranked suffixes.

1288402.4	*i*	33756.55	*ler*
151056.9	*er*	29816.53	*da*
142552.6	*in*	29404.49	*di*
141603.3	*im*	28337.89	*le*
134403.2	*en*	26580.41	*dan*
130794.5	*e*	26373.54	*r*
127352.0	*an*	24183.99	*ti*
113482.6	*a*	22527.26	*un*
82581.95	*ya*	21388.71	*iniz*
78447.74	*ar*	20993.87	*sin*
76353.77	*ak*	20117.60	*ik*
68730.00	*n*	18612.14	*li*
64761.37	*ir*	18316.45	*ek*
53021.67	*la*	...	...
47218.78	*ini*	-38091.8	*t*
44858.18	*lar*	-240917.5	*l*
37229.14	*iz*	-284460.1	*s*

Table 5: Top 30 and bottom 3 extracted suffixes for Turkish. 56881 unique words yielded a total of 175937 ranked suffixes.

4 Experimental Results

For a regular English 1 million token newspaper corpus we get the top 30 plus bottom 3 suffixes as shown in table 4.

English has little affixation compared to e.g Turkish which is at the opposite end of the typological scale (Dryer, 2005). The corresponding results for Turkish on a bible corpus (Tur, 1988) is shown in table 5.

The results largely speak for themselves but some comments are in order. As is easily seen from the lists, some suffixes are suffixes of each other so one could *purge* the list in some way to get only the most "competitive" suffixes. One purging strategy would be to remove x from the list if there is a z such that $x = yx$ and $Z(z) > Z(x)$ (this would remove e.g *-ting* if *-ing* is above it on the list). A more sophisticated purging method is the following, which does slightly more. First, for a word $w \in W$ define its best segmentation as: $Segment(w) = argmax_{s \lessdot w} Z(s)$. Then purge by keeping only those suffixes which are the best parse for at least one word: $S'_W = \{s \in S_W | \exists w Segment(w) = s\}$.

Such purging kicks out the bulk of "junk" suffixes. Table 4 shows the numbers for English, Turkish and the virtually affixless Maori (Bauer et al., 1993). It should noted that "junk" suffixes still remain after purging – typically common stem-final characters – and that there is no simple relation between the number of suffixes left after purging and the amount of morphology of the language in question. Otherwise we would have expected the morphology-less Maori to be left with no, or 28-ish,

Language	Corpus	Tokens	$\lvert W \rvert$	$\lvert S_W \rvert$	$\lvert S'_W \rvert$
Maori	(Mao, 1996)	1101665	8354	23007	78
English	(Eng, 1977)	917634	12999	39845	63
Turkish	(Tur, 1988)	574592	56881	175937	122

Table 6: Figures for different languages on the effects on the size of the suffix list after purging.

suffixes or at least less than English.

A good sign is that the purged list and its order seems to be largely independent of corpus size (as long as the corpus is not very small) but we do get some significant differences between bible English and newspaper English.

We have chosen to illustrate using affixes but the method readily generalizes to prefixes as well and even prefixes and suffixes at the same time. As an example of this, we show top-10 purged prefix-suffix scores in the same table also for some typologically differing languages in table 7. Again, we use bible corpora for cross-language comparability (Swedish (Swe, 1917) and Swahili (Swa, 1953)). The scores have been normalized in each language to allow cross-language comparison – which, judging from the table, seems meaningful. Swahili is an exclusively prefixing language but verbs tend to end in *-a* (whose status as a morpheme is the linguistic sense can be doubted), whereas Swedish is suffixing, although some prefixes are or were productive in word-formation.

A full discussion of further aspects such as a more informed segmentation of words, peeling of multiple suffix layers and purging of unwanted affixes requires, is beyond the scope of this paper.

5 Related Work

For reasons of space we cannot cite and comment every relevant paper even in the narrow view of highly unsupervised extraction of affixes from raw corpus data, but we will cite enough to cover each line of research. The vast fields of word segmentation for speech recognition or for languages which do not mark word boundaries will not be covered. In our view, segmentation into lexical units is a different problem than that of affix extraction since the frequencies of lexical items are different, i.e occur much more sparsely. Results from this area which have been carried over or overlap with affic detection will however be taken into account. A lot of the papers cited have a wider scope and are still useful even though they are critisized here for having a non-optimal affix detection component.

Swedish		English		Swahili	
för-	0.097	*-eth*	0.086	*-a*	0.100
-en	0.086	*-ing*	0.080	*wa-*	0.095
-na	0.036	*-ed*	0.063	*ali-*	0.065
-ade	0.035	*-est*	0.036	*nita-*	0.059
-a	0.034	*-th*	0.035	*aka-*	0.049
-ar	0.033	*-es*	0.034	*ni-*	0.046
-er	0.033	*-s*	0.033	*ku-*	0.044
-as	0.032	*-ah*	0.026	*ata-*	0.042
-s	0.031	*-er*	0.026	*ha-*	0.032
-de	0.031	*-ation*	0.019	*a-*	0.031
...	...	...	...	...	...

Table 7: Comparative figures for prefix vs. suffix detection. The high placement of English *-eth* and *-ah* are due to the fact that the bible version used has drinketh, sitteth etc and a lot of personal names in *-ah*.

Many authors trace their approches back to two early papers by Zellig Harris (Harris, 1955; Harris, 1970) which count *letter successor varieties*. The basic procedure is to ask how many different phonemes occur (in various utterances e.g a corpus) after the first n phonemes of some test utterance and predict that segmentation(s) occur where the number of succesors reaches a peak. For example, if we have *play*, *played*, *playing*, *player*, *players*, *playground* and we wish to test where to segment *plays*, the succesor count for the prefix *pla* would be 1 because only *y* occurs after whereas the number of successors of *play* peak at three (i.e $\{e, i, g\}$). Although the heuristic has had some success it was shown (in various interpretations) as early as (Hafer and Weiss, 1974) that it is not really sound – even for English. A slightly better method is to compile a set of words into a *trie* and predict boundaries at nodes with high actitivity (e.g (Johnson and Martin, 2003; Schone and Jurafsky, 2001; Kazakov and Manandhar, 2001) and earlier papers by the same authors), but this not sound either as non-morphemic short common character sequences also show significant branching.

The algorithm in this paper is differs significantly from the Harris-inspired varieties. First, we do not record the number of phonemes/character of a given prefix/suffix but the total number of continuations. In the example above, that would be the set $\{ed, ing, er, ers, ground\}$ rather than the three-member set of continuing phonemes/characters. Secondly, segmentation of a given word is not the immediate objective and what amounts to identification of the end of a lexical (thus generally low-frequency) item is not within the direct reach of the model. Thirdly, and most importantly, the algorithm in this paper looks at the *slope* of the frequency curve not at peaks in absolute frequency.

A different approach, sometimes used in complement of other sources of information, is to select *aligned pairs* (or sets) of strings that share a long character sequence (work includes (Jacquemin, 1997; Yarowsky and Wicentowski, 2000; Baroni et al., 2002; Clark, 2001)). A notable advantage is that one is not restricted to concatenative morphology.

Many publications (Ćavar et al., 2004; Brent et al., 1995; Goldsmith et al., 2001; Déjean, 1998; Snover et al., 2002; Argamon et al., 2004; Goldsmith, 2001; Creutz and Lagus, 2005; Neuvel and Fulop, 2002; Baroni, 2003; Gaussier, 1999; Sharma et al., 2002; Wicentowski, 2002; Oliver, 2004), and various other works by the same authors, describe strategies that use frequencies, probabilities, and optimization criteria, often Minimum Description Length (MDL), in various combinations. So far, all these are unsatisfactory on two main accounts; on the theretical side, they still owe an explanation of why compression or MDL should give birth to segmentations coinciding with morphemes as linguistically defined. On the experimental side, thresholds, supervised/developed parametres and selective input still cloud the success of reported results, which, in any case, aren't wide enough to sustain some too rash language independence claims.

To be more specific, some MDL approaches aim to minimize the description of the set of words in the input corpus, some to describe all tokens in the corpus, but, none aims to minimize, what one would otherwise expect, the set of possible words in the language. More importantly, none of the reviewed works allow any variation in the description language ("model") during the minimization search. Therefore they should be more properly labeled "weighting schemes" and it's an open question whether their yields correspond to linguistic analysis. Given an input corpus and a traditional linguistic analysis, it is trivial to show that it is possible to decrease description length (according to the given schemes) by stepping away from linguistic analysis. Moreover, various forms of codebook compression, such as Lempel-Ziv compression, yield shorter description but without any known linguistic relevance at all. What is clear, however, apart from whether it is theoretically motivated, is that MDL approaches are *useful*.

A systematic test of segmentation algorithms over many different types of languages has yet to be published. For three reasons, it will not be undertaken here either. First, as e.g already Manning (1998) notes for sandhi phenomena, it is far from clear what the gold standard should be (even though we may agree or agree to disagree on some familiar European languages). Secondly, segmentation algorithms may have different purposes and it might not make good sense to study segmentation in isolation from induction of paradigms. Lastly, and most importantly, all of the reviewed techniques (Wicentowski, 2004; Wicentowski, 2002; Snover et al., 2002; Baroni et al., 2002; Andreev, 1965; Ćavar et al., 2004; Snover and Brent, 2003; Snover and Brent, 2001; Snover, 2002; Schone and Jurafsky, 2001; Jacquemin, 1997; Goldsmith and Hu, 2004; Sharma et al., 2002; Clark, 2001; Kazakov and Manandhar, 1998; Déjean, 1998; Oliver, 2004; Creutz and Lagus, 2002; Creutz and Lagus, 2003; Creutz and Lagus, 2004; Hirsimäki et al., 2003; Creutz and Lagus, 2005; Argamon et al., 2004; Gaussier, 1999; Lehmann, 1973; Langer, 1991; Flenner, 1995; Klenk and Langer, 1989; Goldsmith, 2001; Goldsmith, 2000; Hu et al., 2005b; Hu et al., 2005a; Brent et al., 1995), as they are described, have threshold-parameters of some sort, explicitly claim **not** to work well for an open set of languages, or require noise-free all-form input (Albright, 2002; Manning, 1998; Borin, 1991). Therefore it is not possible to even design a fair test.

In any event, we wish to appeal to the merits of developing a theory in parallel with experimentation – as opposed to only ad hoc result chasing. If we have a theory and we don't get the results we want, we may scrutinize the assumptions behind the theory in order to modify or reject it (understanding why we did so). Without a theory there's no telling what to do or how to interpret intermediate numbers in a long series of calculations.

6 Conclusion

We have presented a new theory of affixation and a parameter-less efficient algorithm for collecting affixes from raw corpus data of an arbitrary language. Depending on one's purposes with it, a cut-off point for the collected list is still missing, or at least, we do not consider that matter here. The results are very promising and competitive but at present we lack formal evaluation in this respect. Future directions also include a more specialized look into the relation between affix-segmentation and paradigmatic variation and further exploits into layered morphology.

7 Acknowledgements

The author has benefited much from discussions with Bengt Nordström.

References

Adam C. Albright. 2002. *The Identification of Bases in Morphological Paradigms*. Ph.D. thesis, University of California at Los Angeles.

Nikolai Dmitrievich Andreev, editor. 1965. *Statistiko-kombinatornoe modelirovanie iazykov*. Akademia Nauk SSSR, Moskva.

Shlomo Argamon, Navot Akiva, Amihood Amit, and Oren Kapah. 2004. Efficient unsupervised recursive word segmentation using minimum description length. In *COLING-04, 22-29 August 2004, Geneva, Switzerland*.

Marco Baroni, Johannes Matiasek, and Harald Trost. 2002. Unsupervised discovery of morphologically related words based on orthographic and semantic similarity. In *Proceedings of the Workshop on Morphological and Phonological Learning of ACL/SIGPHON-2002*, pages 48–57.

Marco Baroni. 2003. Distribution-driven morpheme discovery: A computational/experimental study. *Yearbook of Morphology*, pages 213–248.

Winifred Bauer, William Parker, and Te Kareongawai Evans. 1993. *Maori*. Descriptive Grammars. Routledge, London & New York.

Jerker Blomqvist and Poul Ole Jastrup. 1998. *Grekisk Grammatik: Graesk grammatik*. Akademisk Forlag, København, 2 edition.

Lars Borin. 1991. *The Automatic Induction of Morphological Regularities*. Ph.D. thesis, University of Uppsala.

Michael R. Brent, S. Murthy, and A. Lundberg. 1995. Discovering morphemic suffixes: A case study in minimum description length induction. In *Fifth International Workshop on Artificial Intelligence and Statistics, Ft. Lauderdale, Florida*.

Damir Ćavar, Joshua Herring, Toshikazu Ikuta, Paul Rodrigues, and Giancarlo Schrementi. 2004. On induction of morphology grammars and its role in bootstrapping. In Gerhard Jäger, Paola Monachesi, Gerald Penn, and Shuly Wintner, editors, *Proceedings of Formal Grammar 2004*, pages 47–62.

Alexander Clark. 2001. Learning morphology with pair hidden markov models. In *ACL (Companion Volume)*, pages 55–60.

Mathias Creutz and Krista Lagus. 2002. Unsupervised discovery of morphemes. In *Proceedings of the 6th Workshop of the ACL Special Interest Group in Computational Phonology (SIGPHON), Philadelphia, July 2002*, pages 21–30. Association for Computational Linguistics.

Mathias Creutz and Krista Lagus. 2003. Unsupervised discovery of morphemes. In *Proceedings of the 6th Workshop of the ACL Special Interest Group in Computational Phonology (SIGPHON), Philadelphia, July 2002*, pages 21–30. Association for Computational Linguistics.

Mathias Creutz and Krista Lagus. 2004. Induction of a simple morphology for highly-inflecting languages. In *Proceedings of the 7th Meeting of the ACL Special Interest Group in Computational Phonology (SIGPHON)*, pages 43–51. Barcelona.

Mathias Creutz and Krista Lagus. 2005. Unsupervised morpheme segmentation and morphology induction from text corpora using morfessor 1.0. Technical report, Publications in Computer and Information Science, Report A81, Helsinki University of Technology, March.

Mathias Creutz and Krister Lindén. 2004. Morpheme segmentation gold standards for finnish and english. publications in computer and information science, report a77, helsinki university of technology. Technical report, Publications in Computer and Information Science, Report A77, Helsinki University of Technology, October.

Hervé Déjean. 1998. *Concepts et algorithmes pour la découverte des structures formelles des langues*. Ph.D. thesis, Université de Caen Basse Normandie.

Matthew S. Dryer. 2005. Prefixing versus suffixing in inflectional morphology. In Bernard Comrie, Matthew S. Dryer, David Gil, and Martin Haspelmath, editors, *World Atlas of Language Structures*, pages 110–113. Oxford University Press.

1977. The holy bible, containing the old and new testaments and the apocrypha in the authorized king james version. Thomas Nelson, Nashville, New York.

Gudrun Flenner. 1995. Quantitative morphsegmentierung im spanischen auf phonologischer basis. *Sprache und Datenverarbeitung*, 19(2):63–78. Also cited as: Computatio Linguae II, 1994, pp. 1994 as well as Sprache und Datenverarbeitung 19(2):31-62, 1994.

Éric Gaussier. 1999. Unsupervised learning of derivational morphology from inflectional lexicons. In *Proceedings of the 37th Annual Meeting of the Association for Computational Linguistics (ACL-1999)*. Association for Computational Linguistics, Philadephia.

John Goldsmith and Yu Hu. 2004. From signatures to finite state automata. Technical report TR-2005-05, Department of Computer Science, University of Chicago.

John Goldsmith, Derrick Higgins, and Svetlana Soglasnova. 2001. Automatic language-specific stemming in information retrieval. In Carol Peters, editor, *Cross-Language Information Retrieval and Evaluation: Proceedings of the CLEF 2000 Workshop*, Lecture Notes in Computer Science, pages 273–283. Springer-Verlag, Berlin.

John Goldsmith. 2000. Linguistica: An automatic morphological analyzer. In A. Okrent and J. Boyle, editors, *Proceedings from the Main Session of the Chicago Linguistic Society's thirty-sith Meeting*.

John Goldsmith. 2001. Unsupervised learning of the morphology of natural language. *Computational Linguistics*, 27(2):153–198.

Margaret A. Hafer and Stephen F. Weiss. 1974. Word segmentation by letter successor varieties. *Information and Storge Retrieval*, 10:371–385.

2003 [1999]. Bib la. American Bible Society.

Zellig S. Harris. 1955. From phoneme to morpheme. *Language*, 31(2):190–222.

Zellig S. Harris. 1970. Morpheme boundaries within words: Report on a computer test. In Zellig S. Harris, editor, *Papers in Structural and Transformational Linguistics*, volume 1 of *Formal Linguistics Series*, pages 68–77. D. Reidel, Dordrecht.

Teemu Hirsimäki, Mathias Creutz, Vesa Siivola, and Mikko Kurimo. 2003. Unlimited vocabulary speech recognition based on morphs discovered in an unsupervised manner. In *Proceedings of Eurospeech 2003, Geneva*, pages 2293–2996. Geneva, Switzerland.

Yu Hu, Irina Matveeva, John Goldsmith, and Colin Sprague. 2005a. Refining the SED heuristic for morpheme discovery: Another look at Swahili. In *Proceedings of the Workshop on Psychocomputational Models of Human Language Acquisition*, pages 28–35, Ann Arbor, Michigan, June. Association for Computational Linguistics.

Yu Hu, Irina Matveeva, John Goldsmith, and Colin Sprague. 2005b. Using morphology and syntax together in unsupervised learning. In *Proceedings of the Workshop on Psychocomputational Models of Human Language Acquisition*, pages 20–27, Ann Arbor, Michigan, June. Association for Computational Linguistics.

Christian Jacquemin. 1997. Guessing morphology from terms and corpora. In *Proceedings, 20th Annual International ACM SIGIR Conference on Research and Development in Information Retrieval (SIGIR '97), Philadelphia, PA*.

Howard Johnson and Joel Martin. 2003. Unsupervised learning of morphology for english and inuktitut. In *HLT-NAACL 2003, Human Language Technology Conference of the North American Chapter of the Association for Computational Linguistics, May 27 - June 1, Edmonton, Canada*, volume Companion Volume - Short papers.

Dimitar Kazakov and Suresh Manandhar. 1998. A hybrid approach to word segmentation. In C. D. Page, editor, *Proceedings of the 8th International Workshop on Inductive Logic Programming (ILP-98) in Madison, Wisconsin, USA*, volume 1446 of *Lecture Notes in Artificial Intelligence*. Springer-Verlag, Berlin.

Dimitar Kazakov and Suresh Manandhar. 2001. Unsupervised learning of word segmentation rules with genetic algorithms and inductive logic programming. *Machine Learning*, 43:121–162.

Ursula Klenk and Hagen Langer. 1989. Morphological segmentation without a lexicon. *Literary and Linguistic Computing*, 4(4):247–253.

Peter Ladefoged. 2005. *Vowels and Consonants*. Blackwell, Oxford, 2 edition.

Hagen Langer. 1991. *Ein automatisches Morphsegmentierungsverfahren für deutsche Wortformen*. Ph.D. thesis, Georg-August-Universität zu Göttingen.

Claire Lefebvre. 2004. *Issues in the study of Pidgin and Creole languages*, volume 70 of *Studies in Language Companion Series*. John Benjamins, Amsterdam.

Hubert Lehmann. 1973. *Linguistische Modellbildung und Methodologie*. Max Niemeyer Verlag, Tübingen. Pp. 71-76 and 88-93.

Joanes Leizarraga. 1571. Iesus krist gure iaunaren testamentu berria. Pierre Hautin, Inprimizale, Roxellan. [NT only].

Christopher D. Manning. 1998. The segmentation problem in morphology learning. In Jill Burstein and Claudia Leacock, editors, *Proceedings of the Joint Conference on New Methods in Language Processing and Computational Language Learning*, pages 299–305. Association for Computational Linguistics, Somerset, New Jersey.

1996. Maori bible. The British & Foreign Bible Society, London, England.

David G. Nash. 1980. *Topics in Warlpiri Grammar*. Ph.D. thesis, Massachusetts Institute of Technology.

Sylvain Neuvel and Sean A. Fulop. 2002. Unsupervised learning of morphology without morphemes. In *Workshop on Morphological and Phonological Learning at Association for Computational Linguistics 40th Anniversary Meeting (ACL-02), July 6-12*, pages 9–15. ACL Publications.

A. Oliver. 2004. *Adquisició d'informació lèxica i morfosintàctica a partir de corpus sense anotar: aplicació al rus i al croat*. Ph.D. thesis, Universitat de Barcelona.

Franz Rosenthal. 1995. *A grammar of biblical Aramaic*, volume 5 of *Porta linguarum Orientalium*. Harrassowitz, Wiesbaden, 6 edition.

Patrick Schone and Daniel Jurafsky. 2001. Knowledge-free induction of inflectional morphologies. In *Proceedings of the North American Chapter of the Association for Computational Linguistics, Pittsburgh, PA, 2001*.

Utpal Sharma, Jugal Kalita, and Rajib Das. 2002. Unsupervised learning of morphology for building lexicon for a highly inflectional language. In *Proceedings of the 6th Workshop of the ACL Special Interest Group in Computational Phonology (SIGPHON), Philadelphia, July 2002*, pages 1–10. Association for Computational Linguistics.

Matthew G. Snover and Michael R. Brent. 2001. A bayesian model for morpheme and paradigm identification. In *Proceedings of the 39th Annual Meeting of the Association for Computational Linguistics (ACL-2001)*, pages 482–490. Morgan Kaufmann Publishers.

Matthew G. Snover and Michael R. Brent. 2003. A probabilistic model for learning concatenative morphology. In S. Becker, S. Thrun, and K. Obermayer, editors, *Advances in Neural Information Processing Systems 15*, pages 1513–1520. MIT Press, Cambridge, MA.

Matthew G. Snover, Gaja E. Jarosz, and Michael R. Brent. 2002. Unsupervised learning of morphology using a novel directed search algorithm: Taking the first step. In *Workshop on Morphological and Phonological Learning at Association for Computational Linguistics 40th Anniversary Meeting (ACL-02), July 6-12*. ACL Publications.

Matthew G. Snover. 2002. An unsupervised knowledge free algorithm for the learning of morphology in natural languages. Master's thesis, Department of Computer Science, Washington University.

1953. Maandiko matakatifu ya mungu yaitwaya biblia, yaani agano la kale na agano jipya, katika lugha ya kiswahili. British and Foreign Bible Society, London, England.

1917. Gamla och nya testamentet: de kanoniska böckerna. Norstedt, Stockgholm.

Anthony Traill. 1994. *A !Xóõ Dictionary*, volume 9 of *Quellen zur Khoisan-Forschung/Research in Khoisan Studies*. Rüdiger Köppe Verlag, Köln.

1988. Turkish bible. American Bible Society, Tulsa, Oklahoma.

Richard Wicentowski. 2002. *Modeling and Learning Multilingual Inflectional Morphology in a Minimally Supervised Framework*. Ph.D. thesis, Johns Hopkins University, Baltimore, MD.

Richard Wicentowski. 2004. Multilingual noise-robust supervised morphological analysis using the word-frame model. In *Proceedings of the ACL Special Interest Group on Computational Phonology (SIGPHON)*, pages 70–77.

1968–2001. Bible: selections in warlpiri. Summer Institute of Linguistics. Document 0650 of the Aboriginal Studies Electronic Data Archive (ASEDA), AIATSIS (Australian Institute of Aboriginal and Torres Strait Islander Studies), Canberra.

David Yarowsky and Richard Wicentowski. 2000. Minimally supervised morphological analysis by multimodal alignment. In *Proceedings of the 38th Annual Meeting of the Association for Computational Linguistics (ACL-2000)*, pages 207–216.

Author Index